Ministering to Single Adults

Ministering
to
Single Adults

by

Gene Van Note

CST

Beacon Hill Press of Kansas City
Kansas City, Missouri

Permission to quote from the following copyrighted versions of the Bible
is acknowledged with appreciation:

The *New International Version of the New Testament* (NIV), © l973 by
the New York Bible Society International.

The *New American Standard Bible* (NASB), © The Lockman Foundation, 1960, 1962, 1968, 1971, 1972, 1973, 1975.

Dedication

To

Susan, Karen, Kevin
Young adults who have
brought me joy

Contents

1 / Single Adults: Our Biggest Unmet Challenge   9

2 / Expanding the Church's Vision   24

3 / Single Adults—Who Are They?   41

4 / Building a Base for Growth   55

5 / Alternatives to Marriage   70

6 / Getting Started in the Local Church   89

Reference Notes   107

Instructions for Receiving
Christian Service Training Credit

1. This is the text for First Series Unit 401a, "Ministering to the Single Adult." Six 50-minute sessions, or the equivalent in time, are required.
2. Your class should be registered with the general office at least three weeks before your first class session. This will allow time for the office to get the class report forms, individual registration slips, and credit cards to you. Also, it will help get texts on time.
3. Each pupil must be present for five of the six sessions and read the text to receive credit.
4. Please send the class report in promptly to the Christian Service Training office upon completion of the course.
5. For Home Study purposes, a Study Guide is available and credit is granted when written work has been sent to the general office.

For further information consult your local Christian Service Training director or write...

CHRISTIAN SERVICE TRAINING
6401 THE PASEO
KANSAS CITY, MO 64131

CHAPTER 1

Single Adults:
Our Biggest Unmet Challenge

There is an unmarried adult for every married couple in our country. One-third of the adult population is single. They come in all shapes and sizes, marital history, and economic status. Many are young. For them, life is filled with hope. It is easy to be optimistic. These young people, in the sunrise of their adult life, believe that they will always be as happy as they are now.

But not all single adults are young and beautiful, happy and handsome. Society has most often equated singles with never-married or recently divorced young adults under the age of 30. Their life is portrayed as one that flaunts the historic rules of morality in favor of a sex-oriented existence with pleasure as their goal, and the *Playboy* magazine as their bible. Frankly, many married adults look on their state with a mixture of pity and envy.

That picture is as inaccurate and unfair as the one that questions the sexual orientation of every bachelor, and labels unmarried ladies as "old maids." These convenient symbols are a form of shorthand that not only reduces the need for a person to seriously consider the situation; they hide the real problem from careful review.

The fact is that most single adults are not young and carefree. Nor are they sexual libertarians. They are a composite of the population representing every age, social level, cultural group, and religious persuasion. Many of them have experienced severe tragedy. They have known the death of hope, the death of a spouse, or the death of a marriage. In a culture that honors the young, the glamorous, and the married, they often feel as useful as a fifth wheel or are treated as if they were carriers of the plague.

These people are neither better nor worse than their married counterparts. Their situation, however, is complicated by the fact of their singleness and the factors that brought it about. A small minority of these single adults are in the church. They are happy, well-adjusted people whose spiritual, emotional, and social needs are being met in an atmosphere of acceptance and love.

There are others who also attend church regularly who are not as fortunate. The church is not providing an answer to their problems. They return to their homes with the same loneliness they carried with them to worship, while hiding their personal sorrow behind a charming smile. Except for recent times, and but for special cases, meeting their needs and ministering to their hurts has not been a high-priority item in the average local church. Currently, the majority of the single adult population does not regularly attend church at any time, anywhere. The reasons will be considered later. It is enough at this point to note the relative scarcity of single adults at worship.

I. The Challenge

Single adults, that long-hidden third of the adult population, refuse to be ignored any longer. The largest and fastest-growing minority group in the country, they are gaining visibility at an accelerating rate. Businessmen have discovered them. A careful look at the commercials on television and the ads in popular secular magazines confirms this. Single adults are a multimillion-dollar resource for the business community. A wide variety of products and many new businesses have been created to attract and serve them and their sometimes nontraditional life-style.

That singles are a significant segment of the population, the largest concentrated pool of sales prospects in the nation, is illustrated by the sales record of some key products. In a recent year, more than half of all the Porsche sports cars and 40 percent of all Gremlin subcompacts sold were purchased by single adults. In most metropolitan areas, half of all "Visa" cardholders are unmarried.

"The truth of the matter, as an unmarried Chicago hairstylist puts it, is, 'We work just like anybody else. You have to work to be able to afford to live these days, and I really get tired of reading all those articles about how much fun I'm having.' One tall, pot-bellied, 30-year-old observer added, 'If I had done half the stuff people think I do, I'd probably be dead by now.'"[1]

Nor is there any reason to believe that this phenomenon will quickly fade from the scene. On the contrary, the reverse seems to be more probable. Divorce, just one factor in the rapid rise in the single adult population, is multiplying and shows no signs of tapering off in the near future. Though many divorces are followed by remarriage, there are now so many divorces that this factor alone will, almost inevitably, cause the singles' sector to grow.

Single adults comprise the greatest unmet challenge the church faces at this present time. The reasons for this 20th-century happening and what the church may do to minister to this great group of people, is the subject of this book.

This challenge has two major components. *First,* to create a caring fellowship and design a program that will encourage and enable single adults to become full members of the Body of Christ. *Second,* to express the redeeming love of Christ, and demonstrate an openness to every person so that they will be attracted to the Christ who can bring wholeness and peace to their troubled lives.

That the church is faced with a new challenge will not surprise the careful observer of the current scene, nor will it trouble the devout. The church has always been faced with new opportunities that call forth the best it has to give. The history of the church is filled with the exciting account of how it has met those challenges successfully. As new and unexpected demands have been placed upon the church, it has reacted with imagination and vigor to extend the ministry of redemption to everyone. As the custodian of morality, the church is basically conservative. That is as it should be. But that is not to say that it is static. It has demonstrated itself to be flexible and adaptable, able to meet every challenge to its existence while extending its ministry to meet every human need.

II. Reasons for Growth of the Singles Population

The simplest answer is to admit that there is no simple answer. That is also the most accurate one. However, it is clear that the rapid increase in the number of adults who choose not to marry, or remarry, is a reflection of the changing moral code and a growing permissiveness in our culture. It is beyond the scope of this study to consider the reasons for these traumatic changes, changes that have revolutionized the shape of working society and the family framework. Did a relaxed child-rearing philosophy spawn casual society, or did a so-called "liberated" society open the door for almost unlimited tolerance? The answer is not important. Our desire is not to analyze single adults, but to share the life of Christ with them.

One thing is clear, the American family is under great stress. Part of it is traceable to Henry Ford's lovable monster, the assembly line. As relatively inexpensive transportation rolled off the assembly line, cow trails became county roads and county roads became interstate highways. Once a man knew everyone he met and was known by all who saw him. But cheap and swift transportation has made it easy to become anonymous. We have become a mobile population. Companies transfer their personnel from one end of the country to the other on a routine basis. Families are divided by thousands of miles. Children grow to maturity without experiencing the warmth of a grandmother's love, while their parents struggle with massive problems in a lonely city, unsupported by those who love them most. This is today's family, called by sociologists a "nuclear family," the expression of our impersonal age.

Today's nuclear family is in danger of collapse. The external supports have been removed by our mobility and its inner strength diluted by our practical atheism. Is it any wonder that the modern family has been defined as "two parents, two children, and a psychiatrist"?

This declining morality and disintegrating family life has coincided with one of this century's most powerful forces, "Women's Lib." The Christian Church has nothing to fear from the Women's Liberation movement. In fact, the founder of the Church, Jesus Christ, raised women to a new status, one not known in history prior to that time. This new thrust among women has no moral quality about it, that is to say, it is neither moral nor immoral. However, with its encouragement for women to find their identity apart from marriage and a family, it places an additional strain on the family structure, and suggests another reason for the growing singles population.

All these factors have combined with others not as easily seen, to bring about a liberalization of the divorce laws. "No-fault" divorces are becoming increasingly popular as a greater number of states institute new laws regulating the dissolution of marriage.

Our affluent society provides the time and money for young people to engage in a "search for identity." This coupled with the lack of a military draft is another item in the equation we are constructing concerning the reasons for the growth in the singles sector. All of these have made forms of living together outside of marriage socially acceptalbe, if not religiously permissible. These "alternative life-styles" may have many emotional, spiritual, and legal pitfalls, but there are a multiplying number of couples involved.

Let's review the reasons why one-third of the adult population of North America is not currently married:

1. Changing attitudes toward marriage
2. Liberalization of the divorce laws
3. Declining morality and disintegrating family life
4. Women's Lib movement
5. No military draft
6. Search for identity
7. Alternative life-styles

Care must be taken lest it be implied that there are only negative reasons for choosing not to marry. It has long been assumed in our society that marriage was preferable to the single life. However, for some very good reasons, some people choose to live their lives as single adults. As we shall see in a later chapter, the moral issue is not whether a person is married or single, but how responsibly he lives the life-style he has chosen.

III. The Variety of the Challenge

A divorced mother of two was a leader in the development of a regional singles organization. Letters had been sent from the organizing committee to all of the pastors in the area announcing the first meeting. To assure complete coverage in their publicity, the committee members were phoning each pastor personally.

It was Thursday evening, just following dinner, when one pastor responded to her call by saying, "We don't have any singles in our church."

She was surprised. Surely, she thought, a church with more than 200 in attendance would have some single adults in their fellowship.

She pursued the matter. "You mean," she asked, "that you don't have any divorced people or any widows in your congregation?"

"Oh, yes," the pastor replied, "but we don't have any singles!"

She did not allow his answer to deter her. Gently she helped him to see that he needed to expand his definition of single adulthood to include far more than those young adults who had not yet made their first trip to the marriage altar.

Single adults come in all ages. If you draw a line at age 30, you will have divided the single adult population just about in half. The most recent studies place 46 percent of these people below the age of 30 and 54 percent above.

The largest group of single adults, more than 50 percent, is composed of those who have never married.[2] Many of these could have married but, for personal reasons, decided against it. Others, having been denied the privilege to marry the object of their love, delayed further emotional attachments for fear of failure. These people, expecially the women, face a crisis of confidence in their early 30s.

The remainder of the single adult population is divided among the divorced, the widowed, and the legally separated. The needs, both expressed and unexpressed, vary widely depending on the age and past history of the individual. Obviously, the fact of their singleness is about the only thing a 22-year-old recent college graduate shares with a 40-year-old divorcee or a 71-year-old widower. They are all single adults, but clearly cannot be lumped together in some kind of "catch-all" singles program in a local church. It is this diversity that will challenge the best in creative effort by concerned Christians. The hopeful aspect is that these are adults—mature, experienced adults— with tremendous personal and human resources. Given an opportunity they can develop the program that best ministers to their needs. They do not need sponsors, just a chance!

Throughout our study we will be returning to these separate groups of single adults to look at them in more detail in order to provide the base for ministry. As a foundation to our study we now turn to a quick look at the broad spectrum of single adulthood.

College-Career

This is, of course, the largest group of single adults in our country. They are completing their education, breaking away from the immediate supervision of their parents, and beginning to establish their own lives. They face many problems, nearly all of which are solved by getting a good job and becoming a part of an accepting, caring fellowship. They are optimistic, hopeful. Most of them plan to marry. Some of them have gone through devastating emotional experiences with the opposite sex, but most young adults

16

in this age-group have the capacity to rebound rather quickly and look toward the future.

College-Career young people need the direction of the church in career guidance and adult examples in the church of commitment to Christ and His cause. They are open to the call of Christ and the challenge of the church, while being harsh on hypocrisy and anything that appears to be phony.

The church is probably doing its best work among single adults with those in the College-Career age-group. It is a tremendously important time in life and demands the best that we can give to it.

Young Singles

These young adults are getting established in their jobs or professions. Most of them live in their own apartments, and enjoy the freedom. They are beginning to question whether they will ever marry, and are wondering about the future. These are society's most visible single adults, the ones who buy the sports cars and to whom the singles' ads are focused. Generally speaking, the ages for this group are from 24-35. Some experts suggest that the world of the older single begins for women at age 26 and for men at age 32. While this varies with each individual, the 30th year is an important year in the life of every young adult who has never been married. It signals the need for a new approach to life.

Senior Singles

Almost no attention is given to this group which, statistically, forms one-fourth of all single adults. That is, little attention is given to them as singles. Many churches have very creative programs for senior citizens that include these widowed and divorced people. These are excellent approaches to the problems and opportunities associated with those who have lived beyond their 65th year. It would appear, however, that in most churches the program could well be expanded to give more specific attention to the special needs of these people.

Never Married

Or, single by choice.

We turn, now, away from age-related singleness to status-related singleness. An increasing number of young people are choosing not to marry. Some of these are homosexual, but most are not. They have the same heterosexual drives as the married population, but for personal reasons choose not to marry. A small percentage of these remain in the church. Even a casual glance at the average church's program identifies the reason. In our family-oriented churches there is no place for them to fit comfortably. The "single by choice" adults who remain with the church continue because of the special care and love of some of the perceptive members of a local congregation who include them in rather than single them out.

Formerly Married

This is the term coming into use to identify those who have experienced one of life's most devastating experiences: divorce. Statistically, it is the smallest of the segments of single society. It is, however, the most rapidly growing and probably represents those with the greatest needs, unsolved problems, and unanswered questions.

The growing incidence of divorce has opened up another area of opportunity and responsibility for society and the church—single parents. Currently, one child in every six is living in a home where just one parent is present. Many of these homes have experienced the death of a spouse, but a growing number are the result of divorce.

In Washington state's populous King County, 52 percent of the children in Seattle schools are living in homes where only one parent is in residence.[3] The special needs of both children and parents in these homes will require the highest quality of love the church has to give.

Divorce in both its scriptural and human dimension is a subject that cannot be bypassed or ignored in any study of single adults. We shall take a look at it in chapter 5.

Widowed

Every church has people who have lost their spouses by death. Most churches know how to express their love and compassion at the time of bereavement and for a few weeks following. Probably the great wish of these people is for a continuing interest in the love of the people in the church to help them readjust to a single state. These people, expecially the widows, are often in need of help on a practical level. Job reentry, car repair, house maintenance, as well as a fulfilled social life are basic to the rebuilding of a base for happy Christian living.

Legal Separation

This variety of singleness is no longer common in our society. The changing attitude toward divorce has almost eliminated this procedure. However, there are still some people in our country who have chosen not to get a divorce, but have decided that they cannot live together. These people have special needs for love and affection, companionship and acceptance. Their limited number does not reduce the intensity of the emptiness they experience.

IV. Debunking Some Myths

Modern advertising has made the singles' scene look like fun. For some, it is. It is fun for "the few who are not too homely, too old, too frail, too fat, too skinny, too strapped with financial problems, too insecure, too plagued with acne, crooked teeth, or myopia, and too far removed—by the demands of their jobs, schools, geography, or their own discomfiture with an 'endless summer' in a world beset by poverty, injustice, and disease—to fit precisely into the carefree, glossy, technicolor world of ads and movies."[4]

That is another way of saying that the singles' scene is often different when lived from the inside than it is when viewed from the outside. A new single in California makes these humorous, but all-too-true observations. Single men everywhere will find it easy to identify with his experience:

1. Not one thing will move.
2. An empty wastebasket does not exist.
3. A dishwasher's basic function is to get things lost.
4. Soaking certain matter loose requires more time than there is.
5. A five pound ham lasts.
6. Doing one thing at a time is quite enough. But there is never only one.
7. There is no reasonable place to put anything that is flat and limber.
8. Lids don't fit anything. But if they did, build more cupboards.
9. A shopping list has no end.
10. One alone doesn't sleep much.[5]

This calls into question the myth put into epigrammatical form, "A married man may have a better half, but bachelors have better quarters."

Here are some popularly held assumptions about the single state. None of them are universally true. They do not apply to single adults any more than they fit married couples. To understand single adults and minister effectively to and with them we will have to get beyond these myths:

1. *They have more money than most couples.* The reverse is more commonly true. Child support, paying for family expenses on reduced income, etc., all identify this myth as patently false and unkind. In reality, nearly one-fourth of all widows fall below the poverty line.

2. *They have more time than most couples,* therefore, should have more time to give to the church. Actually, they may have less time, especially if they are single parents.

3. *There is "something wrong" or they would get married.* In fact, they may have exhibited more strength by not getting into an improper marriage than some in their age-group showed by getting married out of the will of the Lord.

4. *They are "swingers" or have an abnormal sexual orientation.* This is not only untrue for most singles, but where this myth is dominant it short-circuits the ministry of the church.

5. *Children from single-parent homes are doomed to be less capable and more disturbed.* While divorce is admittedly a devastating experience, recent studies show that if a child lives with a parent who loves and cares for him, he does as well in school as children from two-parent families.

6. *Singles have a well-rounded social life and are happier than most married couples.* The reverse is most often true, particularly in the church. Most of the social life for adults in the church is structured along two-parent family lines. Single adults are often left groping for companionship. It is a statistical fact that married people live longer than those who remain single. National Health Census

data points out that people of all races and of both sexes die earlier in life if they are single. For example, white bachelors under the age of 65 experience fatal heart disease and cancer at twice the rate of married men the same age. For some single adults, the only way they can escape from isolation is to get sick. It is evident that people die from loneliness. Six of the eight leading causes of premature death are clearly linked to our behavior, says psychiatrist James J. Lynch. "Yes," he concludes, "many people die from loneliness."

V. A Place to Begin

Death, divorce, personal choice—whatever the reason for a person's single state—he must not allow his loss, or lack of, to define the dimensions of the future. Many single adults are immobilized by their unfulfilled dreams. Our society has encouraged them to play a "waiting game" until they are married and can really begin to live.

Single adults should be encouraged to build today the values and life-styles they want to be a part of their lives in the future. As Linda LeSourd says, "Investing time and creativity in making a present house or apartment a home helps establish for them a much-needed sense of security and identity apart from marriage. Living with others and having to share meals, responsibilities and possessions forces their personal and spiritual growth."[6]

Singleness can be a significant experience. It can, and ought to, be a time of preparation. If it is, and if marriage should come, then they can enter into marriage with greater personal resources, a depth of purpose and maturity that will give the marriage greater chance of success. It is a time to prepare to live.

But it is also a time to be, to live in the *now*. One of the most exciting things the church can do for single adults is to get them out of a "holding pattern" where they are waiting for the right matrimonial runway, into the happy experience of living for Christ in the present.

SOMETHING TO DISCUSS OR DO

1. Why are there so few single adults in the church?

2. What are some of the negative stereotypes that married people attach to single adults?

3. What proportion of the adult population is made up of single adults?

4. What is the dual challenge facing the church in its ministry to single adults?

5. Name some reasons for the rapid growth of the singles population.

6. List the different categories of single adults and a characterizing feature of each group.

7. Review the myths about single adults' life-style and identify the one(s) you are guilty of believing. Resolve to change your thinking.

CHAPTER 2

Expanding the Church's Vision

Look in on your adult Sunday school classes; observe carefully the worship services; recall the last major social event in your church. Were one-third of the adults who attended those events unmarried? If the answer is Yes, you are to be commended and are excused from reading the remainder of this chapter. The chances are, however, that you will read it. You are already aware of the importance of an effective ministry to single adults and will want to improve and expand that ministry.

On the other hand, if the total number of married persons participating in your church events is significantly greater than two-thirds of the total, then this chapter will contain important information for you.

Why the one-third, two-thirds relationship? Simply this: one-third of the adult population in North America is not currently married. If the total number of single adults who regularly attend your church activities is considerably less than one-third of the total, then your church is not ministering adequately to the largest minority group in your community.

A new subculture has become a part of the current scene. Single adults are everywhere, representing all ages, ethnic backgrounds, religious preferences, and job classifications. It is easy to presume that singles are just adults in transition, and many of them are. But not all of them are waiting for marriage, postponing everything until they make the trip to the altar and the promised golden life of connubial bliss. They are deeply involved in every part of our society.

The size of this new cultural subgroup has forced society to change its attitude toward singleness. Not long ago, a popular book on premarital counseling declared, "Absolute proof of femininity requires that a girl not only marry to prove that she is attractive to men but also that she conceive and bear a child. If she cannot perform both of these functions, she is thought to be an incomplete person."

But things are different now. Singleness has been accepted as a viable life-style. Laws have been changed, granting single adults, especially single women, greater freedoms and more equitable treatment. No longer is divorce an automatic barrier to advancement in politics or business. Credit granting procedures have been changed and employment applications revised to remove the stigma of singleness. The business sector has expanded its product offerings and services to attract the interest and money of single adults. New forms of recreation, entertainment, publications, and housing have appeared. There are singles' apartments, singles' bars, singles' weekends in the Bahamas, even a singles' wardrobe for the contemporary man.

The changing singles' scene is illustrated by what has happened in the area of divorce. Prior to the beginning of this century divorce was relatively uncommon. In 1900, there were only 55,751 divorces granted in the United States, or 4 divorces per 1,000 married couples. But in 1950 there were 385,000 divorces, or 10 per 1,000 married couples. 1964 statistics reveal 428,000 divorces compared to

1,720,000 marriages, or about a four-to-one ratio. There is nothing in more recent statistics to indicate a reversal of the trend; rather, an acceleration of the problem is evident.[1]

All this has occurred in conjunction with a growing permissiveness in sexual behavior. For a great many people, the restraints against premarital, and extramarital sexual intimacy have been removed. Sexual experiences between consenting adults are judged, by many, to be acceptable and even "good" if "they do not hurt anyone." Intimacy for pleasure without commitment is being promoted as a proper form of expression for the unmarried. More effective forms of birth control, especially "The Pill" have provided the technology that has aided this disintegration of moral values.

One result of all this change has been the emergence of "alternative life-styles," a modern term used to identify a wide variety of "living together" arrangements. Alternative life-styles have been given both community approval and legal sanction. In many jurisdictions, single adults can adopt children. The courts have ruled that couples who "live together" accept certain legal responsibilities for each other, especially if there are children from that union.

The rapid growth of the single-adult population is troubling, liberating, and/or challenging depending on who is observing, and who is being observed. In the midst of it is the church. Slowly it is altering its preoccupation with a family ministry to see the great group of single adults that live in the community it serves. It is significant that the churches which are developing a redemptive ministry to single adults have had the courage to look at themselves without being defensive. That is not easy, but it is the first important step in reaching single adults for Christ, and supporting the Christian single adults who are currently a part of the fellowship.

26

I. THE CHURCH AS SINGLE ADULTS SEE IT

A. The Church's Traditional Attitude Toward Singleness

Take a big step away from your deep involvement in the program and ministry of your church and try to see it as it is seen by single adults. If your church is an average congregation, and most churches are, what you see will be troubling, and ought to cause you to seek reevaluation of the priorities in your redemptive approach to your community.

Where are most single adults on Sunday morning?

Answer: Somewhere except in church!

Unfortunately, most single adults do not attend church, your church, my church, anyone's church!

> To hear singles—encountered at poolside, at singles' bars, in bus stations, in counseling sessions, anywhere but church—tell it, church is the last place where they can experience a sense of "belonging." . . . Where are the singles on Sunday morning? The answer is disarmingly simple. Almost any place where they can experience a sense of peace and contentment on their "day of rest" in a nonthreatening environment, where they can "fit in" without having to endure the hostile stares or uncomprehending sermons of those to whom their unmarried state is an aberration and a threat, wherever they are welcomed with open arms and without reservations, or, at least, left in peace.[2]

Pastor Nicholas Christoff, a Lutheran minister with an extremely successful apartment ministry to single adults in Chicago, makes this observation about the place of singles' bars, "The bar is a place where singles can, if they choose, submerge their identity and the problems gnawing at them in the laughter, the music, the tinkling of ice in glasses, and the camaraderie of strangers—without jeopardy to their professional standing or self respect." He continues with these words of tremendous challenge to the church, "For many, the singles bar even performs a function that was once thought to be within the exclusive purview of the church and family life. 'I find that a night with old friends, or spent making new ones, is a tremendously regenerative type of experience,' says Bart, a Washington, D.C., bachelor engineer. 'It recharges my batteries for the week ahead.'"[3]

If that be true, and a great many single adults believe that it is, then the church ought to take a look at itself to see what it is that makes the church unattractive to singles.

The church's traditional attitude toward singles begins with the advice that Christian leaders give to young people. The Church has proclaimed that everyone faces three major decisions in life: Master, Mission, and Mate. Or, to put it another way, the message is that everyone must decide whether or not they will allow the Lord to become the Master of their life, what vocation they will follow, and whom they will marry. But what if by choice, or the lack of it, a person has answered only the first two questions? What if the third choice is "still pending"? In a group that has mandated marriage as the "scriptural way" to Christian fulfillment and personal happiness, they are made to feel incomplete, and sometimes, even out of the will of God.

Nancy Hardesty notes, "If the Catholic heresy is to say that celibacy is a more Christian life-style, then the Protestant heresy is to say that marriage is the only, or the better life-style, or the only way one can be complete."

Some unfortunate titles and terms have been used in the church that illustrate this restricted view of human development, such as the WARM Class (Women and Reluctant Men), The Misfits, or SCOUP (Single, Career, and

28

Obviously Unattached Persons).[4] Really, now, would any of those titles encourage you to attend church if you were placed in those categories?

Couple that with the tendency of many in the church to question the attractiveness, the sexual orientation, or the moral quality of anyone who chooses to remain single.

Many single adults could easily relate with the divorced mother of two young children. Less than 30 years of age, the death of her marriage had come a few years earlier, but not all the pain had disappeared. The divorce had left her without the emotional equipment to deal effectively with life. She did not know what to do or to whom she could turn for help and advice. For a long time she did not do anything that was very important, submerged in a strange, new feeling.

Finally, she diagnosed her condition. She was, to use her own words, "just feeling kinda temporary." She had neither goals nor dreams; only her responsibilities to her two children kept her going from one day to the next. Like thousands of others in her situation, she was reacting to life rather than participating in it.

Having been reared in the church, she turned there for help at this time of personal crisis. She visited a church in the neighborhood and felt good. The worship renewed many happy memories of her childhood. Obviously, the Lord was present. There were many indications that He was blessing the people who were members of that fellowship.

But she was not part of it. The worship services were rewarding, but every Sunday was the same. She walked to her car feeling very much alone, certain that no one cared. The fellowship of the church did not seem to include singles.

Finally, she talked with the pastor, who encouraged her to make some friends. He said, "The people in the church do not know how to handle the fact of your divorce. They do not know what to say to you. You will need to break the ice."

So, she did, She "broke the ice," made some friends, and now is happy in the church. She is aware that they love her, and is being helped by the atmosphere of honesty and caring that exists. But it happened only after she took the initiative.

There was no note of anger nor chastisement in her voice, just a haunting question, "When a person goes to church looking for friends, should she be the one who is asked to 'make friends'?"

"Because of divorce and our pain, the churches could not handle the problems with singles," writes one formerly married church member. "Gradually we were lost from their protective friendships. We were not easy people to love. We hurt in too many places and pain is not easy to look upon. We were the Gethsemanes and Calvaries of Christ."[5]

"When things like this happen, and they do, is it any wonder that single adults feel that they have been relegated to second-class status in the church? It was in that mood that one single commented, "It is easier to be a single outside the church than inside, because outside no one questions the validity of my singleness."

B. The Tension Created by the Church's Emphasis On A "Family Ministry."

Let it be clearly stated and strongly affirmed at this point that the church has an obligation to uphold the sacredness of marriage and the value of a Christian home. Both are under severe attack. The church dare not relax, even a tiny bit, in its redemptive ministry to families.

The trouble comes with, and for, those who do not fit

into the traditional mold: happy, two-parent families with an adequate income, acceptable social status, and loving, obedient children. That is just another way of saying that as the church moves into comfortable middle-class it finds it increasingly difficult to adapt itself to those whose life is filled with tragedy, heartache, and any significant deviation from the norm. It is easier to exclude those who do not "fit in." Often, and tragically, that exclusion is not a deliberate "counting out," but a careless unawareness that does not include the single adults "in."

This is illustrated by the single parent who wrote the following letter:

> I write this for the hundreds of lonely Christians. Don't get me wrong. I love my Lord with all my heart. He has dominion over everything in my life, especially for the last 15 months when He was good enough to forgive me for what I'd done. Through a beautiful church family and a wonderful minister and wife I have grown spiritually and happily.
>
> Oh, there's a lot I don't understand, but He does, and maybe someday I'll understand why I have to write what I'm writing.
>
> I think it is because my church family doesn't understand. I am happy in the church, but have you ever thought how much it would mean to all of us "single parents" if you would say, "Hey, how about a cup of coffee with us tonight?"
>
> We realize we are different and maybe it makes you uncomfortable. But we are also children of God who have a special need, a need for being in a loving atmosphere. We need to know we are "cared for."
>
> I walked through my church tonight watching all the happy couples going to each other's homes, or somewhere, for coffee and no one stopped to think I was crying inside.
>
> Ask me.
>
> O Lord, help them know we are lonely through the loss of a spouse through death or divorce. We are people in need of caring, at least once in a while.

I wonder if you know when you fail us. You are happy. You are married. I know you think the Lord completely fills our lives, and He is my Love and my Life. But, like Him, we are human with needs. Our main need is love . . . your love.

Six months passed.

Another letter arrived. It was bittersweet. She was too timid to tell her church that she was lonely and they were too busy to notice. When the Christmas holidays made her singleness unbearable, she sought companionship in a singles' bar. She met a man. A relationship followed, promising love and companionship, but resulting in remorse, guilt, and multiplied loneliness. She found forgiveness, but closed the letter on the less than hopeful note that her Christian friends seemed more ready to criticize than provide companionship. She mused how long she could continue without a friend.

That is the church as seen by many single adults. Does it represent your church?

II. The Church Single Adults Would Like to See

A. A Church That Is Developing a "Single Eye"

Many concerned churchmen would like to reach single adults with the message of salvation and surround them with the caring fellowship of loving Christians. They are frustrated by their inability to find a "handle," a way to get hold of this kind of ministry.

Perceptive single adults believe that the "handle" is acceptance and love. Shirley Close writes,

> Single women bear another type of vulnerability. That is of being scrutinized simply for their singleness. This type of skeptical, and often condescending, analy-

sis comes from all realms of society, but perhaps more predominantly from the church . . . I tried various singles groups in different churches and had a great deal of difficulty feeling comfortable there . . . What is it, then, that I needed? How could the church minister both to my soul and to my social needs? Quite by accident, I was invited to be the alto soloist at a church in my community. Since I was a poverty-stricken graduate student I accepted, thinking that if it became unbearable, I would leave. From the first day I entered the choir room of that parish, I was totally enveloped by a genuine acceptance. No matter who I was, where I came from, or where I was going, they loved me unreservedly. There was never a sense of condemnation or fear of my marital status, life, or career goals. Instead they reinforced those areas with their supportive love. When I was struggling through a difficult time, they struggled with me and vice versa. This particular church did not meet every possible need, but for the first time ever, I felt the reciprocal love from an entire congregation.[6]

This highlights the primary desire of single adults in relation to the church. They want to be accepted as persons of worth, totally apart from their marital status; to be included as full members of the fellowship right now, not at some future time when they fit more neatly into the prevailing cultural framework. They are saying,"We want to be a part of the church, not only to receive, but also to have the opportunity to give!"

Single adults want, and need, the chance to participate in every aspect of the church program. It may be that their apparent lack of concern is the result of being disfranchised. Actually, in most churches, teenagers have more representation on the official board than is given to single adults.

The development of a "single eye," a consciousness of singles' concerns, will take seriously the words of the Mennonite theologian John Howard Yoder, "It needs to be taught as normative Christian truth that singleness is the first normal state for every Christian. Marriage is not wrong, and existing marriages are to be nurtured. Yet there exists no Christian imperative to become married as soon as one can or to prefer marriage over singleness as a more whole or wholesome situation."[7]

This growing awareness of singles' concerns, their needs, hopes, and dreams, will include a consideration of the subtle, and sometimes not so subtle, discrimination against single adults in the church. Often the church's programmed events exclude single adults, such as "Couples' Retreats" and "Sweetheart Banquets." Or, announcements that read: ". . . and spouse." Or, those that note the cost will be, "$5.00 couple; $3.00 single," as if it cost the hostess 50 cents extra to set a plate for a single person. At the same time, compassionate churches will make a deliberate choice not to become a religiously oriented dating service, nor a "marriage factory" for singles.

Acceptance does not mean automatic approval.

> There are some ethical concerns involved in an authentic ministry with single adults, such as a biblical understanding regarding divorce and remarriage and a healthy understanding regarding sexuality. We must love persons in the midst of various life-styles. Ministry must be approached from a particular stance, and there is no need to apologize for that stance. However, it is also biblical to love persons wherever they happen to be, rather than if they move to the spot we have designated for them.[8]

Acceptance means a commitment to help the person whatever their circumstances and need.

Here are three proposals generated by different parts of the church community that seek to meet this challenge. They are given as illustrations of what beginning steps are being made. The first is the "Seattle Task Force," a group

34

of pastors and other professionals working with single adults in Seattle, Wash. They make these recommendations:

1. Affirm the fact that adult singleness is a reality in our culture.
2. Highlight singles as a part of the worshiping community with a special liturgical celebration.
3. Be sensitive to the use of discriminatory labels often used in referring to singles (i.e. "broken home," "swinging single," "gay divorcee").
4. Rethink the biblical-theological meaning of singleness in the light of today's society.
5. Develop a pastoral outreach based on the distinct needs of singles that goes beyond "crisis care."
6. Seek to integrate the single into the love and community of the church family.

In preparation for their special year-long emphasis toward ministering to single adults, the Southern Baptist Convention has issued this "Single Statement":

1. A single adult ministry which lasts and grows is one in which Sunday morning Bible study has a central focus.
2. A caring atmosphere in single adult Sunday school enables singles to share, to learn, and to find community.
3. The application of Sunday morning Bible study should be a catalyst for single adults to strategize and carry out ministry with other persons.
4. Calling attention in a positive way to the presence of single adults in the church may help some married persons to reassess negative stereotypes of singleness.
5. While the general needs and developmental tasks of single adults are no different from those of mar-

ried persons, the options for meeting these needs through single adult Sunday school are different.

6. Single adults need to feel and to be an accepted, contributing part of the total church community.
7. The most important factor about a single adult is his name.
8. Negative feelings expressed and accepted in a single adult Bible study group lose their destructive power.
9. Respect for differences among single adults proves a single adult Sunday school worker cares.
10. The most important ingredient in a nurturing relationship is honesty.

Another approach to this opportunity is represented in "The Singles Manifesto" prepared by "The Singles Task Force" of the California Conference of the United Methodist Church. It is as follows:

Singles call upon the church to be aware of the many single persons who are in the church and community, together with the varieties of singleness (never married, divorced, widowed), and:

1. To recognize singleness as a legitimate life-style and an acceptable status.
2. To affirm persons who are single through choice or circumstance by structuring church activities and programs to be inclusive rather than exclusive (not family or age-oriented only).
3. To develop within the life of the church support structures uniquely designed to meet the needs of single persons and/or one-parent families.
4. To be aware that single persons need to FEEL and BE a part of the whole church's struggle to become a *family*.
5. To be aware that single persons are ready to share their gifts and talents as a part of the total ministry of the church.

36

6. To recognize the injustice and inequities that single persons experience in economic, social, political areas of life, and become involved as an agent of change. (E.g.: Taxes, credit, leisure activities, and social attitudes.)

7. To develop a theology which deals with divorce as a fact of life and recognize divorced persons and one-parent families resulting from divorce as acceptable persons who need love and support.

8. To become aware of cultural stereotypes which tend to assume marriage as the only acceptable life-style. (E.g.: "When are you going to settle down?" "It's too bad a nice person like you isn't married." "Too bad about your divorce; what did he/she do?" "Aren't you two getting married yet?" "Come to the potluck; we'll find someone to sit with you.")

These can be summarized in this statement: single adults request that the church be built on Jesus Christ and not on families. This will enable each person to be accepted as a worthy individual regardless of his marital status and incorporated into the life and ministry of the church on the basis of his God-given talents and spiritual gifts. It will, also, recognize the special needs of single parents and one-parent families.

B. A Redemptive Ministry to Single Parents

"Becoming a single parent is like giving birth to a barbwire fence—extremely painful," writes Virginia Watts. Yet, she says, that is not the end. "It is also the beginning of a new you, and the journey into which you have been thrust will include many positive experiences."[9]

The church has a beautiful opportunity to share in that journey. People, in their adult life, are most open to the church and its message during periods of crisis and change. For this reason, the Body of Christ has an unparalleled privilege to share in the trauma, and hopefully the triumph, that come to these people in intense pain.

The matter of divorce is not the key issue. God has clearly decreed the sacredness of marriage. The fact is, however, that people are divorced and will continue to "split the blanket," to use a colorful phrase to identify a tragic experience. The focus of the church's ministry to these broken people is not a theological treatise on the evils of divorce, but a healing ministry of love and care. It must be directed toward meeting genuine needs, designed to re-build self-worth and renewal in Christ.

As Keith Miller notes, "Strangely, the problem is almost worse for Christians. We are subtly trained that if we are really restless or lonely, it may be a reflection on the depth of our commitment. So we repress these feelings and are conscious only of a strange franticness, or even boredom, or lack of interest in Christianity—which also can produce guilt."[10] This phenomenon has caused some to observe that the most difficult place in life to be totally open and honest is in church! A caring, redemptive fellowship can bring healing to people who have suffered such disruptive, tearing experiences. It will take at face-value, without rejection, all who feel the need to pray with the honesty expressed by one single parent who wrote this prayer to God,

> I write this to You, God, with the hope that You will understand.
> I feel lost, separated, and totally alone, and yet, there are many close by. I wonder where I can find the happiness and peace of mind I so desperately want. I need the closeness and total caring of another being, and yet the ones for whom I care are incapable of caring for anyone but themselves.
> I have the children, and that should be sufficient, but after they are in bed, the loneliness and need are much more than I can take.

Please help me, God, to find the peace I so desperately need and the wisdom to know how to handle it when I find it.

God, help this feeling of emptiness to be filled with other things which are of value to both myself and my children.

Help me not to grab for just anything to fill the loneliness and help me to realize my importance to myself, my self-confidence, as I seem to have lost them along the way.

Guide me with people as I seem to reach for the ones who can hurt me the most. When I reach for those whom I allow to hurt me, hold me tightly and help me to pull away from them and closer to things which are truly important.

Teach me that to be alone is not the worst thing in the world. Help me to realize this, as this is my biggest problem.

Loneliness makes me frightened of the future, regretful of the past, and dissatisfied with the present—help me to fill this void.

Help me to erase my desire to seek revenge on those who have hurt me, and replace it with a forgiving spirit, realizing I may have hurt others, and I myself need forgiveness.

And, dear Lord, help me to learn to trust again. Amen.[11]

The church that responds redemptively to needs like this will have caught the vision of the "extended family" of the church.

C. A Recognition of the "Extended Family" of the Church

One single adult noted that, in the time of crisis, his needs were met, not by the church, but by people in the church. It was not an administrative expression of institutional concern but the unstructured expression of love and support. He had become "a part of the family." A ministry to singles will include this authentic Christian fellowship. Many of the experiments in intimacy are the searching individual's wish for acceptance. "For two years," an attractive woman said, "I've been looking in all the wrong places." After only one evening with a caring group of Christians she saw the difference.[12]

For the church, this means, if necessary, a move away from a preoccupation with self-preservation by adopting a willingness to take a risk with people. For single adults, the building of an "extended family" will require a willingness to commit themselves to others, once again. Unfortunately, many singles live at the level of contingency, not commitment. They, too, must respond in a mutual effort of "family" building if the extended family of the church is to minister to their needs. Out of it can come a creative, growing group of Christians who through their mutual support will find new ways to become more like Christ.

SOMETHING TO DISCUSS OR DO

1. List four ways in which the church has estranged single adults by its traditional attitude toward them.

2. How has the church's emphasis on a "family ministry" affected its relationship with single adults?

3. What do single adults want more than anything else from the church?

4. Discuss the relationship between "acceptance" and "approval" of the single adult in the church.

5. How should the church deal with the problem of divorce in order to meet the needs of these hurting people? Why has it failed in ministering effectively to the divorced?

6. Discuss the meaning of "the extended family."

CHAPTER 3

Single Adults—Who Are They?

Historically, single adults have been called bachelors, old maids, and a variety of other unkind terms. They were identified by what they appeared to lack—a spouse. If they achieved fame people seemed surprised that anyone so crippled could do anything important. After all, they were unmarried!

Of course, there were some things worse than being an unmarried adult: typhoid fever and catatonic schizophrenia are two that come quickly to mind!

"Normal people get married" was the cultural refrain. Mothers were confident they had completed their matronly mission if their children "married well." In fact, a happy marriage, or at least the photo of a smiling family, was an essential part of every political campaign. If a legislator was divorced while in office he rarely ran for reelection, for defeat at the polls was a certainty.

Now throughout North America politicians are continued in office whose homelife is a shambles. Some are even considered for significant promotions after highly publicized extramarital affairs.

We have come a long way from the time when unmarried people were not considered trustworthy, to the place where we are willing to trust world leadership to those whose morality is severely compromised.

In the meantime, the public attitude has swung from questions about the normalcy of unmarried adults to suspicion about their sexual reliability. This doubt about their morality has been fueled by the entertainment media and glossy ads in popular magazines.

The truth is that both extremes are inaccurate and unfair. Society is discovering that an individual can be a whole person, though unmarried. A spouse does not guarantee success, nor does marriage insure happiness. Some of life's loneliest people do not go home to a vacant studio apartment. Rather, they lie awake in bed listening to the relaxed breathing of their sleeping spouse and wonder how they could have been so blind when they said to the preacher, ". . . for better or for worse."

It may be that the most significant event in a church's preparation to minister to these people comes when they refer to them as single adults instead of unmarried folks.

I. WHO ARE THEY?

A. They Are People

Single adults are just like a cross section of the adult population, because that is exactly what they are. First and foremost they are people. They have all the abilities and agonies common to mankind. They possess the same power for good and potential for evil as every other son and daughter of Adam's race. Tell them a joke and they laugh, cut them and they bleed, hurt them and they cry, crush them and they die. They are not animals to be led and fed, nor are they statistics to be studied. Single adults are flesh and blood human beings with the same drives and dreams common to married couples. The choice not to marry does not make a person subhuman any more than a marriage license makes him superhuman.

B. They Are Adults

Most significantly, these people are adults, full-grown, mature, responsible adults—not overgrown nor ancient teenagers. Two things are important when you think about adults:

1. There is greater variation between adults than there is between persons at any other clearly defined period in life. A vivacious college cheerleader, a glowing bride, a harried mother, an efficient real-estate broker, a relaxed grandmother, and a senile old lady are all adults. Actually, these may be periods in life experienced by the same woman in her adult years.

Obviously, the needs of the individual at each level will differ greatly from the other stages. A bouncing cheerleader and a wheelchair-bound senior citizen may share some key things: their womanness, their adulthood, and perhaps even their singleness. Yet that 74-year-old lady will have more in common with other women in their retirement years than she shares with the 21-year-old college student.

This does not mean that these two age-groups can never be combined. One vigorous single adult group plans several meetings each year with the senior adults in their church to everyone's joy and mutual benefit.

All this, and more, points up the second key fact about adults,

2. It is not a static experience. We believe this to be true about young adults to the extent that we fracture the family finances to purchase a college education for them.

A full ministry to single adults will recognize this as

also true for nearly all levels of adult experience. It is this possibility of change, of growth, that gives the Christian message its reason for being. People in all walks of life, at all ages, on the rebound from every shattering experience, can change. One older man caught the power of this when responding to a question from a friend he had not seen for several years. "Since I talked with you last," he reported with characteristic humility, "I know I am closer to 'the measure of the stature of the fulness of Christ'" (Eph. 4:13).

The fact of their maturity is far more significant than specifying their marital state. Thus it is a helpful approach to ministry to consistently identify them as *single adults,* not just as *singles.* The former title highlights their achievement, the latter a state many feel represents incompleteness. Some Sunday schools are beginning to structure their classes along the lines of "Married Adults" and "Single Adults" to insure that no one is overlooked in their planning and that everyone is recognized in a positive way.

C. They Are *Single* Adults

This is the focus of our study. Singleness is the dominant fact of their life, as much as marriage is for couples. There is freedom and there is fear, liberty and loneliness.

Keep in mind that everyone is single by choice. It is true that there is a greater number of women in our society than men. As people grow older, this statistical variation becomes even greater, until in their retirement years there are three women for each man.

But do not let the statistics fool you. Everyone who wants to get married can get married—that is, if getting married is more important than anything else. The only reason some people are married is that they were willing to make unfortunate and highly regrettable choices that were outside the will of God for their lives. The church should be as supportive of those who decide not to marry contrary to God's will as it is to those who follow His call to missionary service. People who act, at great personal sacrifice for high moral principle should be honored, not relegated to second-class status.

It has been suggested that there ought to be, in the church, a ritual similar to ordination confirming a person in his or her singleness. One is wont to suppose, however, that such a ritual would go largely unused. Most single adults anticipate that they will marry, or, at least, do not want to irrevocably close the door against the possibility. One recent poll reveals this. When a group of single adults were asked to respond to the question, "How do you see yourself 20 years from now?" 75 percent replied, "Married."

Preoccupation with the fact of their singleness and the normal desire for marriage can steal peace and contentment from single adults. The church has a delightful opportunity to help them see themselves as persons of value and worth totally apart from their marital state. The central focus of the program should be on helping build authentic relationships that will enable people to become mature Christian individuals. "The task we face," writes Walter Trobisch, "is the same whether married or single: To live a fulfilled life in spite of many unfulfilled dreams."

One young lady in her early 20s caught the magnificence of this spiritual insight in this letter to a friend:

I saw my mistake this morning when I was reading I Peter, comparing how much Peter understood when he wrote this letter that he did not understand in the early days of his discipleship. His misunderstanding was his preoccupation with his inheritance in the kingdom, believing it would be a political kingdom. Now he writes to believers to tell them of our inheritance that awaits us, kept undefiled, guarded by God himself.

I don't expect a political kingdom as Peter did, but I do have expectations of what it will mean to me to personally know Christ. I saw this morning that I am trying to live and grow into a redeemed life, but trying to do it with unredeemed hopes and expectations. God helped me this morning to see that my biggest enemy in growth is my own set of expectations of what Jesus must do for me. Like give me a husband.[1]

Those words, "trying to live and grow into a redeemed life, but trying to do it with unredeemed hopes and expectations," establish a point of beginning in the ministry to single adults. God does not intend for anyone, married or single, man or woman, boy or girl, to live a life that is a dull reflection of His glory. There are no second-class citizens in His kingdom. The life of single adulthood is not a life of sublimation and compensation because the good things belong only to the married. It is God's plan to "give good things to them that ask him" (Matt. 7:11).

In that spirit we will look more closely at the world of the single adult. Not as if it were a course in anatomy dissecting a corpse, but sharing in the life that He gives to all who walk with Him.

Adulthood, as someone has noted, is a lifetime sentence. It begins where the teen years end and continues until death. You cannot be promoted to another grade. Once you arrive you are an adult the rest of your life.

There are, of course, different levels or stages of adulthood. Any division for analysis tends to be artificial. However, these categories provide a convenient place to begin. We will view the world of single adults from two different perspectives:

1. Age-group division
2. Experience-related differences

46

II. Age-Group Division

Our study will consider single adults in these age brackets:
1. College/Career: post-high school—23 years of age
2. Young Adults: 24-34 years of age
3. Turning the Corner: 30-40 years of age
4. Middle Adults: 35-54 years of age
5. Pre-retirement: 55-64 years of age
6. Senior Adults: 65 and above

A. College/Career: 18-23 Years of Age

These are the most visible single adults in the church. They have graduated from high school and have either enrolled in college or found a job. Also included in this group are those in military service. This specialized ministry to young people away from home is extremely important. Many churches near military bases have exerted life-changing influence on countless young lives.

1. *Where They Came From*

It is important to remember that the College/Career group is just out of high school. Most churches expend considerable energy and money to provide spiritual guidance for teenagers. The total teen program reflects the highest per capita "people" part of the church's yearly budget. Parents in policy-making positions on church committees and boards give their support to the development of attractive youth programs.

These high school students have a common identity, a bond of mutual interest that cements the group together: their school attendance. They share in the excitement of athletic contests and the depression of final exams. This "herd instinct" is heightened by their universal desire to break away from the parental control they experienced during childhood. Consequently, high school students are influenced more by their peer group than by their parents. Yet nearly all of them are subject to some kind of parental guidance. Parents establish rules of behavior, finance their activities, and provide most of the transportation.

The teen program, in most local churches, is vital and challenging. It is supported by district teen activities providing camps, retreats, and events that are designed to encourage Christian growth and church attendance. Effective teen groups generally have high quality leadership by young people themselves. Most often, teens in leadership come from families that are a vital part of the total church program.

Then comes graduation.

2. *Where They Are*

Immediately following high school graduation, significant changes begin to occur that become conspicuous the following fall. If finances permit, children from strong Christian homes are encouraged to attend a church college. Many of them will respond. The result is that historic teen leadership has suddenly vanished; they have gone off to college.

Two groups remain: *(a)* those who attend a secular college locally, and *(b)* those who get a job and go to work. Rapidly the areas of common interest between these remaining groups grows smaller and smaller. Those who attend college become increasingly interested in the campus scene, and often in parachurch organizations operating on or near the campus. The others, those who are working, are on a totally different time schedule, and share few things of interest.

Commonly, those who do not attend a church college have not been at the core of the teen group in high school.

When this happens, the College/Career group must develop new leadership if it is to survive. The gaps left by the departure of the core group may have additional implications. Often those who remain have attended the church functions because of their friendship with someone in the core group. They may find it difficult to develop new relationships in the group of sufficient meaning to cause them to continue to attend. With the core group gone, there are a smaller number of concerned parents sitting on official boards and committees. There is usually a drastic reduction in money spent on this group as compared with that spent on the teens.

When this is combined with increased independence and financial ability on the part of these young adults, it is easy to see how successful teen programs can crash, offering nothing for the College/Career group.

3. *Where to Begin*

A ministry to College/Career young adults does not begin with either program or curriculum materials. It begins with a person, a concerned, optimistic, happy Christian. What is needed is a person who can bring the remnant together, identify them and help them relate to one another. This leader needs to have enough maturity to deserve respect while providing the bridge enabling these young people to cross into adulthood. Few positions in the church offer the happy rewards that come to the one who works with these dynamic young people.

More attention has been given the characteristics and needs of this group than will be allotted to the other age-group divisions. Their specialized concerns will not be considered anywhere else in this book. Our study will help us see the remainder of the single adult population from several different angles. Thus our age-group examination will be relatively brief.

B. Young Adults—24-34 Years of Age

Earlier, we noted that these are society's most visible single young adults. It is important to note that they are not the most visible group of single adults in the church. In fact, in a great many churches, they do not exist. For reasons already considered, single young adults have not been attracted to the church. They tend to be quite independent, continually searching—in relation to their job, where to live, and what to believe. They gravitate away from rural areas to the attractions and anonymity of the cities. Even there they do not find roots. They are the most mobile part of our population. Paradoxically, they react against the depersonalization of the crowd while struggling to be accepted by and adapting to the demands of the crowd.

As they search for their own identity they are caught in the tension between what they are experiencing and what they were taught as children. Considerable guilt, both pseudo and real, results from their choices. These young adults are looking for the door that opens up on life's good things. They are not sure where it is, but are confident that they will find it.

Obviously, there are tremendous differences in this age-group. At the bottom end they may be at war with the established society, while at age 35, they have made their peace and joined it.

C. Turning the Corner—30-40 Years of Age

Among the games that young people play is the one about love and marriage. The rules dictate that you steadfastly affirm that you will never marry, while you confidently expect the time will come when you will. During the 20s, as one's adult life begins to take shape, marriage is always a viable option. However, it is not overlaid with urgency. Well-meaning people share phrases like, "There is a boy for every girl," or "There are lots of pebbles on the beach." These are intended to indicate that marriage is inevitable.

For some, the time comes when they must be realistic. They must face the fact that marriage is increasingly unlikely. When this happens will vary with each individual, though the thirtieth year seems to be a critical one for a great many single women. The crisis, for men, may come a few years later. But whenever it comes, sometime in their fourth decade single adults must come to grips with the situation and admit that they may never marry.

This is, usually, a greater crisis for women than for men. Single women may become frustrated and bitter, sometimes depressed, because they did not, or could not marry. It is an interesting fact that most divorced women in their thirties eventually remarry, while a decreasing number of the never-married women take their first trip to the marriage altar.

The never-married man is viewed differently from the unmarried woman. The bachelor, in his thirties, is considered "eligible," "a good catch," because he is reasonably secure financially. Women in the same age-group are too often thought to have failed to develop the necessary qualities to attract a man. The career woman is not treated as kindly by society. Marriage and parenthood is expected of them far more than from men who choose not to marry.

Some of the single adults in this situation will need care and understanding as they are guided to establish new goals for their lives. For the success of the group, these people probably should not be placed in positions of leadership while they are in this period of transition.

D. Mid-life—35-54 Years of Age

These people represent the quitest, but most active single adults in the church. They are busy in their jobs or vocations and, those who attend, are usually involved somewhere in the church program. They have experienced both joy and sadness and have triumphed over much of it. They are willing to accept and demand less from life than they did earlier. Maturity has brought a measure of peace.

But it has also brought a new awareness of their lonesomeness. No longer at war with the world, and feeling the need for human companionship, single adults in this age-group may be the most open to the church of all those being considered. It is easy to overlook the needs of these people because they have learned to hide their hurts and repress their feelings. Many of them face a crisis of loneliness or finance. The divorced or widowed may have heavy family concerns and no one to help them share the burden. The fear of growing old alone will begin to enter their consciousness. Though they make few demands, they may represent the most needy sector of the single adult population.

Unfortunately, a meaningful ministry to single adults in this age group is the last to be developed. In some respects they have the greatest needs. Many of them are leaving their home church in search of a congregation where they feel both welcomed and needed. Because it is difficult to develop a program with a small number of participants, a growing number of single adult organizations are being formed with this group as both the catalyst and the nucleus. Many of them represent churches from an entire metropolitan or geographical area. These people will not drain the energy or finances of the church. They need only to be given an opportunity coupled with the understanding and full support of the church.

E. Pre-retirement—55-64 Years of Age

Most of the material available for counseling people in these transition years will also apply to single adults. Obviously, the advice on marital adjustments is not relevant, but they share the same health, housing, and financial needs.

They do, however, face them alone. Often they have less money they can use for retirement planning. Many of them have been unable to purchase a home. These limitations increase their level of apprehension when they pause to review the future.

F. Senior Single Adults—65 and Above

It is easy to list some of the primary concerns of senior adults: aging, inflation, loss of companionship as friends die, fear of death, diminished strength, separation from loved ones, preoccupation with personal needs.

The single senior adult faces all these—alone! He needs encouragement to live, vigorously and victoriously. In most cases senior singles are not helped by specific programs that "single them out." They need the full fellowship of everyone in their age-group, whether married or not.

It may be that some short workshops, or day-long sessions, on their specific needs and interests would be gladly received. Practical sessions on financial planning, or how to handle grief, might provide helpful answers to some very big questions.

CONCLUSION

Our brief review of single adults by age has highlighted one aspect of the challenge: the great variety of interests and needs among them. Obviously, there are experiences that have had a greater impact on them than the passage of time, divorce and death, for example. These experience-related differences will be discussed in a later chapter.

The reason a person is single must be combined with his chronological age to fully understand his needs. Consequently, compassion will always be more important than curriculum in any ministry to single adults.

SOMETHING TO DISCUSS OR DO

1. What one preoccupation can rob a single adult of contentment and peace?

2. How can the church help the single adult to deal with this preoccupation in a constructive and creative manner?

3. List the age-group divisions of single adults, and some identifying characteristics of each group.

CHAPTER 4

Building a Base for Growth

A Bible Study of 1 Corinthians 7

The Bible is almost totally silent about the acceptability of singleness as a way of life for Christians. There are some beautiful Old Testament stories about single adults, such as the love expressed between Ruth and Naomi. Yet this tender story ends with Ruth's happy marriage, not a continuation of her singleness.

The reason is clear. The Jews taught that marriage was an obligation, not an option.

"If a man did not marry and have children, he was said to have 'slain his posterity . . . to have lessened the image of God in the world.'

"Seven were said to be excommunicated from heaven, and the list began, 'A Jew who has no wife; or who has a wife but no children.' God has said, 'Be fruitful and multiply,' and, therefore, not to marry and not to have children was to be guilty of breaking a positive commandment of God."[1]

In ancient Israel, the family was the basis of society. The family continued to hold this central place in the time of Christ. Their total culture—social, political, and religious—was built on the family. Some of the most significant rituals were celebrated in the family circle. The Passover, for example, was distinctly a family experience.

Thus, a common proverb of Christ's day read, "A bachelor is not truly a man at all." Celibacy was thought to be almost a disgrace, though a person could choose this way of life as a vocation to grant himself more free time to serve God. Christ thus fitted into this option in a manner acceptable to His generation.

It is easy to see why the Bible speaks so seldom about single adults.

But Jews were not in the majority in Corinth. There may have been a few Jews in the congregation, but most of them were Greeks trying to follow Christ in one of the cesspools of the ancient world. The Corinthian church reflected the racial and social mixture of the city and, thus, was greatly influenced by the moral decay of this great metropolitan center.

The old Greek city of Corinth was destroyed about 150 years before Christ and rebuilt by Julius Caesar. It drew its importance from its strategic position as the center of trade and military control on the narrow neck of land between the Aegean and the Adriatic Seas. It soon developed into a center for the adventurers, entrepreneurs, and outcasts of the Roman world. This vigorous, cosmopolitan city became the target for the Christian Church under the apostle Paul.

Yet for all its obvious advantages, Corinth seemed to be unlikely soil for the Christian gospel to take root. The city was dominated by the Temple of Aphrodite situated on a stone mountain 1,500 feet above the city. Thousands of temple prostitutes were the priestesses for the worship of Aphrodite, the goddess of love. What a contrast to 1 Corinthians, chapter 13!

Athens had a reputation for culture and learning. Corinth was famous for its corruption. To live "like a Corinthian" was a contemporary phrase signifying a life of luxury and sexual license. It is obvious why Paul, who spent 18 months in Corinth, emphasized that the body of the believer is the temple of the Holy Spirit (1 Cor. 3:16).

The Greeks' view of life was totally different from that of the Jews. These concepts, and the locale, laid the groundwork for the Bible's clearest statement about singleness.

In Greek thought there was a strong disposition to despise the body and anything related to it. This leads to one or the other of two courses of action:

1. "The body is unimportant; therefore, it makes no difference what you do with your body." John, in his first letter, dealt with this heresy which teaches that there is no sin related to the actions of the body.

2. The reverse can also spin off this basic belief. The physical drives are powerful and often lead to experiences that are emotionally devastating. Thus, some Greeks said, "The body is evil. We must bring it under complete subjection. We must obliterate all the natural desires that are a part of the human body."

Both positions had their proponents in Corinth. The first was the more common one, giving support to the incredible immorality that saturated the Corinthian culture. Perhaps in reaction, the second position was taken by some Corinthian Christians. They believed that if you were to follow Christ, you had to deny every physical passion.

It is in that context that the apostle Paul deals with the dual questions, "Should a person marry or remain single?" and "What are the implications of either choice?"

First Corinthians, chapter 7 is unique. It stands alone as almost the Bible's only word on singleness. It was written in response to questions the Corinthians had been asking the apostle.

"Now for the matters you wrote about," Paul continues (1 Cor. 7:1, NIV. All scriptural quotations are from NIV).

Paul's friends in the church raised six questions, some of which reflect the Greek tendency to regard the physical side of existence as evil. These questions are:

1. Should married couples continue normal sexual relations after their conversion? Paul answered, Yes (vv. 1-7).

2. Should single adults marry? Paul prefers the single life for himself, and suggests it as the best course for others, but only if they are able to exercise the required self-control (vv. 8-9).

3. Is divorce between Christians permissible? No (vv. 10-11).

4. What about a Christian whose spouse chooses not to confess his or her faith in Christ? The Christian is to continue in the married relationship unless the pagan partner wants a separation (vv. 12-16).

5. This question is a bit more difficult to define. Probably it is, "Should engaged couples marry?" This is left to the individual, but in the troubled times facing the church, Paul suggests that it will be easier for single people to work out their Christian priorities (vv. 25-38).

6. May widows remarry? Yes, but under the qualifications listed by the apostle (vv. 39-49).[2]

Our purpose in this chapter will be to discover the eternal principles revealed in 1 Corinthians 7 that will help in the development of a mature Christian life as a single adult.

There are three key principles underlying the words of Paul in chapter 7:

A. There are human commitments that conversion does not change.

58

B. There are human tendencies that have a profound effect on the life-style we choose.

C. There are human experiences that mold our ministry, or define the boundaries of our service for the Lord.

A. There Are Human Commitments That Conversion Does Not Change

This is an intensely practical section where Paul does not hesitate to speak directly to the challenge of living a pure life in a morally dirty city. He does not run from the problem in some theological treatise nor hide behind some doctrinal fog. He comes to grips with life as it is being lived by average people in their community. He recognizes both the uniformity there is in the Christian faith and the challenging diversity there is in people. Thus he makes it clear:

1. *The Aptitude for a Specific Mode of Living Is a Gift from God* (note vv. 7-8, 17, 20-24)

Experts disagree as to Paul's earlier marital state. Probably it does not matter, This much is clear, from the time of his first appearance in the Scriptures he is obviously a single adult. His entire Christian ministerial career is built on the options made possible by his singleness.

Characteristically, he feels that his situation is best for everyone. "I wish that all men were as I am . . . Now to the unmarried and the widows I say: It is good for them to stay unmarried, as I am" (vv. 7-8).

Paul is happy with his singleness. It gives him a freedom to serve the Lord that marriage would have denied him. His awareness of the future has convinced him that it is the better of the two options, but he is sensitive enough to know that it is not the best for everyone. He affirms this in these words, "But each man has his own gift from God; one has this gift, another has that" (v. 7). Though he advises singleness, he would rather see a couple marry than face moral crisis or degrade the message of Christ. (vv. 8-9).

Paul wants it clearly understood that Christianity is not intended to be an intolerable burden. It is to bring freedom, peace, and release. Christ does not make carbon-copy Christians from some master plan. There is room for a beautiful diversity of expression that reflects the gifts given to each believer.

There are a few places like Corinth in our world. A Christian couple traveling on the European continent left their hotel to see the city. Ignorant of the area toward which they were walking, they suddenly became aware of the blatant pornography that surrounded them. Explicit pictures of sexual perversion were on display in the shop windows, there was open solicitation for prostitution though they walked together, the curtainless windows of a busy brothel hid nothing that was happening inside.

They were astounded, embarrassed, stunned. They left the area as quickly as they could, but its impact was burned on their souls.

Corinth was like that.

Most of the places where we live promote illicit sex with more finesse, but the temptations are just as real, and sinful gratification is just as readily available.

Paul's advice to the Corinthian Christians is still valid, in Barclay's words, "Examine yourself and choose that way of life in which you can best live the Christian life, and don't attempt an unnatural standard which is impossible and even wrong, for you being such as you are."[3]

2. Married Christians Have Specific Responsibilities

Paul was a single adult by choice. He was a single adult in a religious culture that mandated marriage even more than the church does today. Yet he associated freely with married people. He was the houseguest of Aquila and Priscilla for 18 months in Corinth, working with them in the tentmaking business. Subsequent letters from Paul indicate that they remained two of his closest friends.

The apostle wrote about marriage from the standpoint of observation, if not personal experience. Paul never would have said, "Marriage is a fine institution, but I'm not ready to be committed to an institution." He held marriage in the highest regard.

He was aware of the impact of the sensual Corinthian society. "It is good for a man not to marry. But since there is so much immorality, each man should have his own wife, and each woman her own husband" (vv. 1-2).

"Now to the unmarried and the widows I say: It is good for them to stay unmarried, as I am. But if they cannot control themselves they should marry, for it is better to marry than to burn with passion." (vv. 8-9).

If this seems like a poor reason for marriage and a low view of its purpose, join it with Paul's picture in Ephesians where he compares proper marital love with Christ's love for the church. In a morally corrupt society, Paul wants Christians to be very careful lest improper sexual behavior would tarnish the message of Christ.

Thus he lists these basic responsibilities Christian couples have to each other:

a. Married Christians are not to get a divorce (vv. 10-11).

b. Christian couples have certain obligations to each other. He mentions two in particular: sex and time.

Clearly, there were some Christians in Corinth who had "spiritualized" their marriage. Deeply affected by the Greek idea that the body was evil they denied the bodily desires in order to be "Christian." Paul declared that except for short periods, with mutual consent, married

Christians are to maintain a healthy sexual relationship (vv. 3-5). "Do not deprive each other except by mutual consent and for a time, so that you may devote yourselves to prayer. Then come together again so that Satan will not tempt you because of your lack of self-control" (v. 5). Paul would make it clear that Christianity does not deny the proper, healthy expression of the God-given emotional drives common to every person.

Married Christians have a responsibility to spend time with one another and plan their lives to include each other (vv. 33-35).

But not every married Christian has a Christian spouse. What then?

3. *Christians Married to Unbelievers* (vv. 12-16)

Anytime the church as a successful evangelistic ministry in a pagan society there will be many occasions when one spouse becomes a Christian while the other remains an unbeliever. This troubled the infant church in Corinth. What should the believing partner do when faced with that dilemma?

The apostle divides the problems into two sections: a mixed marriage where the two partners are content (vv. 12-14); and a mixed marriage where the unbelieving partner is not happy (vv. 15-16).

a. A mixed marriage where both partners are content (vv. 12-14). In the first example it is apparent that neither spouse wants to terminate their marriage. Paul instructs that the believing spouse has an obligation and a privilege to remain with the non-Christian partner. The difference in religious belief and loyalty does not constitute grounds for separation.

There is a companion thought that has exciting implications. It goes beyond the realization that there is no spiritual stigma attached to the Christian whose spouse does not follow the Lord. It is that the marriage benefits from the Christian faith of even one of the partners. Both the unbelieving spouse and the children can become better because of the Christian virtues lived out in the experience of the one who loves the Lord. "For the unbelieving husband has been sanctified through his wife, and the unbelieving wife has been sanctified through her believing husband" (v. 14).

The Christian spouse continuing as a part of a pagan family has the rare opportunity to share Christ with them. Many a family has become totally Christian because of the quiet, effective faith of just one member. That kind of Christian love can develop into a family tradition of the kind that became evident when a Sunday school teacher asked one child, "Why do you love God?"

"I don't know, sir," he replied, "I guess it just runs in our family."

b. A mixed marriage where the unbelieving partner is not happy (vv. 15-16). This is the opposite of the earlier example. "If the unbeliever refuses to remain with the believer, the Christian is free from obligation to sustain the marriage: **But if the unbelieving depart, let him depart.** In this way the believer comes into **Peace.** Under these circumstances the Christian is not committed to a lifetime of persecution, abuse, and agony because of his relationship to a heathen partner. . . . Peace and love should always be the trademarks of Christian living."[4]

4. *Slavery: Religious or Human* (vv. 18-23)

Christianity is far more than a radical revolution that smashes institutions and people. It is a vital, positive force that gives new life and a new reason for living.

In relation to religious rituals that would stunt Christian growth, Paul recommends that they be discarded in favor of new life in Christ. "Keeping God's commands is what counts," he concludes.

The slave is commended to freedom. "If you can gain freedom, do so" (v. 21). But not even this should be allowed to destroy one's faith in God nor one's witness in the community. The exciting companion truth is that growth, change, and personal improvement are a vital part of the Christian experience.

Now we come to one of the two main concerns of this chapter toward which the apostle's argument moves unerringly.

5. *Singleness*

"Should a person marry or remain single?"

The foundational truth on which all of Paul's reasoning is based is this: Christian faith is not related to a person's marital state. (Note these verses: 2, 7, 8-9, 17, 20, 32-35, 38.)

There is a phrase in the ancient words that form the traditional wedding ceremony, "We are gathered together . . . to join this man and this woman in holy matrimony, which is an honorable estate."

No thinking person, certainly not Paul, would deny that. But he would also insist that "singleness" is also an honorable estate.

The apostle in 1 Corinthians 7 wants it understood that there are valid reasons for remaining single. There were valid reasons then. There are valid reasons now.

Singleness is an honorable estate.

The Jewish religious tradition mandated marriage. A proselyte to Judaism would be under great pressure to marry and raise a family.

There is no similar religious pressure for the convert

64

to Christianity to get married. Paul makes it clear that this decision is the private privilege of every believer.

With the privilege of choice there are, however, certain inevitable responsibilities. The opportunity to choose carries with it the inevitable implications of those choices. Consequently, the apostle affirms,

B. There Are Human Tendencies That Have a Profound Effect on the Life-style We Choose

This is Christianity with its feet in the mud, not its head in the clouds. Never is Christ's message more redemptive nor more disruptive than when it walks the streets. Thus Paul becomes intensely practical while discussing the key issue, "Should Christians marry?"

First, he wants it clearly understood that this is an extremely personal issue that may change from time to time for each individual Christian. What was God's will at one period in his experience may not be God's will at a later time.

Early in this chapter Paul writes, "Now to the unmarried and widows I say: It is good for them to stay unmarried, as I am" (v. 8). But later he observes, "So then, he who marries the virgin does right, but he who does not marry does even better" (v. 38).

Clearly the individual's personal reaction to the allurements and temptations of his cultural situation is a vital issue here. As has been noted earlier, Paul understands that it is not God's plan for everyone to marry, nor for everyone to remain single—". . . each man has his own gift from God; one has this gift, another has that" (v. 7). Each Christian is to make his decision relative to marriage partly on the basis of his own personality—his strength and weakness.

Marriage or singleness, should, however, be regarded

in the light of God's plan for our lives and service, "What I mean, brothers, is that the time is short" (v. 29). It is evident that:

C. There Are Human Experiences That Mold Our Ministry

The choice to marry or to remain single will define some of the boundaries of Christian service.

1. *A married couple must give attention to each other and to their family* (vv. 3-5, 10-14, 33-34).

It is both tragic and unchristian for a person to spend so much time in doing things for the church that he neglects his family. This is a special danger faced by those who are deeply involved in the ministry of the church and its various programs.

2. *It is for this reason that Paul advises that the unmarried people in Corinth choose not to marry.*

He is convinced that Christians do not have long to proclaim the message of redemption. "What I mean, brothers, is that the time is short" (v. 29). A married couple must spend a major portion of their time in relation to the interests and needs of the family. A single adult can, in an emergency such as described by Paul, "live in a right way in undivided devotion to the Lord" (v. 35).

Marriage, for the devout follower of Jesus Christ, must be built on something far more significant than mutual interest and sexual attraction. The engaged couple will give careful consideration to how they can more effectively serve Christ together than they would be able to serve Him singly (vv. 32-35). Thus Paul takes the issue of singleness out of its cultural and religious context and gives it a new dimension. Each person must decide the leading of the Lord for himself in relation to his humanity and God's commission for his life.

3. *In that regard, and in recognition of the society of which they are a part, Paul insists that Christians willingly accept the sexual responsibilities and limitations of the life-style they choose.*

Married couples will honor each other by being responsive to the very real emotional needs that are a part of the human condition (vv. 2-5).

Single Christians will not engage in sexual activities prior to, or outside of marriage. This is clearly implied in Paul's advice in verses 1-2, and 7-9.

Conclusion

The secret of effective Christian living is for each believer to select the life-style that fits his or her personality in accordance with God's will. In recent years genetic experimentation has generated considerable discussion concerning "cloning"—the laboratory reproduction of living beings. The biological theory concerning cloning suggests that it is possible to take the genes of one living being and use them to build another living creature. This new being, called a "clone," would be identical in every way with the original. There are many religious implications to "cloning" that we do not have time to discuss here. It is significant, though, that the apostle Paul wants to make it clear that the Lord is not in the business of "cloning" Christians. There is a remarkable variety in human personality that continues through conversion and gives the church variety and depth.

Thus the key question is not, "Are you married or single?" but rather, "Are you in the center of God's will at this point in your spiritual journey?"

Helen was 26 years of age, unmarried, and just beginning to make some measurable progress in her professional career. Previously she had been engaged to be married, but that relationship had been severed for quite some time. As a single young adult she was convinced that it was just a matter of time until she became a single middle adult.

"Everything I did revolved around the fact that I was not married," she commented later. "One day I woke up to the fact that everything I had done for years, every decision I made, revolved around my fear of being single. I was terrified that I would be single the rest of my life.

"Finally, I gave my singleness to the Lord. I decided that if I was ever going to be happy I had better get started. I told the Lord that I wanted His will more than I wanted to get married. For the first time in years I was happy."

She wrote her former fiance about her new commitment to Jesus Christ. He responded positively. No longer wrapped up in her problems and consumed by her fears, she became more attractive. Two years later they were married.

She made these observations about her new life: "I'm glad I got married, but it wasn't exactly what I expected. I thought I would be so happy that it would solve all my problems. I find that my level of happiness is about the same as before I got married." She shared some of the frustrations and new obligations that came with her marital state and then concluded, "I'm happily married, and happy married, but it wasn't marriage that made me happy." Her mature decisions and Christian commitment would have brought a smile to the face of the apostle Paul.

Something to Discuss or Do

1. Describe the moral tone of the city of Corinth at the time Paul wrote his letter to the Corinthian church.

2. Identify the two schools of thought about the human body that prevailed in Greece when Paul wrote to the Corinthian church.

3. Review the six questions to which Paul addresses himself with regard to singleness, marriage, and divorce. Review his answer to each.

4. What are the three key principles underlying Paul's words in 1 Corinthians 7? How does Paul enlarge upon these principles as they apply to marriage and singleness?

5. How can a Christian single adult best approach the prospect of living single for the rest of his life?

CHAPTER **5**

Alternatives to Marriage

The key question is not, "Are you married or single?" but rather, "Are you in the center of God's will at this point in your spiritual journey?" This is, as we noted in the previous chapter, the central thought in Paul's argument on the validity of the single life.

To admit the acceptability of singleness does not downgrade marriage. Not everyone will marry, some cannot, others choose to remain single for sublime reasons. "God's creative intention gives dignity to marriage, but His redemptive actions place limits on marriage. Jesus said that there were some, including himself, who would never marry for the sake of the kingdom (Matthew 19:21). Thus, Jesus is the model of morality for the unmarried."[1]

Others may never marry the object of their love for reasons that are more practical than noble. When one matron tried to comfort a young lady with the words, "Someday you'll meet the right man," she replied, "I've met him already. I knew he was the right man. Unfortunately, he didn't realize it."[2]

Some single adults are able to accept their status with a disarming sense of humor. One of them was regularly encouraged by this motto: "A man can make a fool of himself without knowing it—but only if he is single."[3]

70

We have seen that singleness among adults has many facets and dimensions. Some of them, having never exchanged nuptial vows, know nothing of the married life. In contrast are the recently singled adults who were married for so many years that they cannot recall what it was like to be unmarried. Others married early, going from the security of their parents' home to a similar dependency on their spouse.

Then, abruptly, they are single again. As Virginia Watts observes, "Our minds and bodies do not automatically push a button which says MARRIED or SINGLE. After being married for one year, or for twenty years, we continue to think *married*. . . . Just as it took time to adjust to being married after being single for so many years, it will be difficult to adjust to being single after being married."[4]

However, an increasing number of people are having to discover what it means to become single again. Alvin Toffler accurately reflected the current situation when he wrote in his best-selling book *Future Shock*, that traditional marriage is proving less and less capable of "delivering on its promise of lifetime love." He concludes, "To expect a marriage to last under modern conditions is to expect a lot. To ask love to last indefinitely is to expect even more. Transience and novelty are both in league against it."[5]

Too pessimistic?

Perhaps. But the evidence suggests that we are headed pell-mell toward that situation—if we have not already arrived!

This changing attitude toward the marriage covenant is reflected in the phrase being substituted in some modern ceremonies. In place of "till death do us part," the couple repeats, "till love do us part." Marriage, for them, is not intended to be a lifelong commitment. Rather, it is a contract to be kept in force only as long as deemed mutually satisfactory by the participating partners.

The church, which has until recently ostracized the divorcee while vehemently condemning divorce, now can easily see the tragedy up close. A perceptive evaluation of recent statistics indicates that couples who share strong religious beliefs have fewer divorces. There are, at the same time, reasons to conclude that increased marital happiness has not been the inevitable result. Family stress, separation, and divorce are becoming far more common among evangelical Christians. It is the rare congregation that has not experienced its impact at the core of its fellowship. Divorce, unfortunately, is a part of the life of nearly every church. There can be few self-righteous islands of pharisaical "purity" left.

In short, what we are trying to say is that the church must get past its preoccupation with titles and stereotypes. It must grow beyond its fear of being tainted by those whose history or life-style does not reflect the accepted norm before it can develop a redemptive ministry to them.

This chapter will take a closer look at what it means to be single in a couples' world in these three sections:

I. Divorce and Remarriage
II. Death—Those That Remain
III. The Bible and Human Sexuality

I. Divorce and Remarriage

Divorce is a word with which we must learn to live, but we do not have to like it—or approve. It is easy to laugh about it, as the comic does when he says, "Divorce occurs when the husband decides that he is too good to be true!"

That is clever, but it hides the hideous truth. Divorce is like death, only sometimes death would be easier. There are times when there would be fewer problems to have the clergyman say, "Earth to earth, ashes to ashes, dust to dust," than to hear even the most compassionate judge say "Divorce granted!" When was the last time you heard a divorcee say, "Going through divorce has been so much fun, I hope I can do it again, soon!" More characteristic is the woman in a Divorce Recovery group. The leader was encouraging the participants to accept the reality of their divorce as the first step in growth and spiritual renewal.

"Repeat after me," he requested. "Say these words, 'I am divorced.'"

Before he could finish the sentence, one woman, divorced just eight days, burst out, "I can't say that," and the tears washed her face.

The person next to her reached out in compassionate understanding and said, "Don't give up. Time will help."

Abruptly, she was interrupted by another lady whose crisp words revealed a not easily forgotten anger. "It takes more than time. I've been divorced eight years and if I'd known what it was going to be like, I would have worked harder to keep my marriage together."

There seems to be no reason for the church to approve divorce as a legitimate expression of the Christian faith when so few divorced people themselves support it and believe in it. Couple this with the strong biblical message against divorce, and it seems clear that the church ought not to weaken its historic stand.

While it is becoming increasingly easier to legally dissolve a marriage, the trend toward liberalization has not diminished the emotional and spiritual cost. "Divorce is seldom, if ever, the casual, gleeful, legalized mate-swapping some people envision it. Few people are so unfeeling about a relationship rooted in love and entered into with high hopes. A more realistic idea of the personal cost of divorce is suggested by the titles of two articles which recently appeared in *Redbook,* 'The Myth of Civilized Divorce' and 'It's Never a Nice Divorce.'"[6]

There are no factors common to all divorces. Some marriages come apart because the internal stress is greater than the bonds of matrimony. Others are torn apart by external forces, causing a weak union, or a union of weak people, to collapse. Immaturity, jealousy, selfishness, and many other character traits and deficiencies may combine to hinder any attempt to save the marriage.

The fact is, most marriages could be saved if both husband and wife were willing to make the necessary adjustments. Perhaps the only exceptions are those where perversion, or serious psychological problems exist. Clearly the church should be more diligent in supporting those redemptive ministries to couples that will aid them in developing healthy Christian homes.

There seem to be three stages to divorce. First, an emotional divorce occurs while the couple share the same household. Arguments, insensitivity, harshness, erode the joy that they once knew. This is followed by a denial of physical contact, especially for happy purposes. During this period, they have a physical separation when one of them moves out.

Men and women respond differently to divorce. Our culture teaches men to be tough, to deny their feelings. In crisis situations, they tend to run from their emotions or submerge them in a flurry of experiences.

Women seem to go through a far greater crisis of identity than men. They must search for meaning apart from the man whose name they and their children carry. Financially, it often results in drastic changes of life-style for both of them as the same income must now support two households instead of one. Many times women are forced back on the job market after years of child-rearing. This, too, can take an awesome emotional toll.[7]

A recent study showed that divorced people:

—ate and slept more erratically
—found money to be a major point of disagreement
—experienced self-doubt over their lack of ability to transcend failure
—saw more of their children after divorce (25 percent of the men)
—became more strict with the children after initial leniency
—experienced continuation of same conflicts they had in the marriage
—yearned for long-lasting relationships after initial fling
—were dissatisfied with their new social life
—drifted away from old acquaintances
—felt trapped (especially the women) by child-rearing responsibilities[8]

Divorce is a cataclysmic experience that may be a positive good in a small minority of situations. But for most people, divorce is failure. They have not been able to achieve in the most sublime venture open to mankind. Earlier, he, or she, made some major commitments, fully intending to keep them. But now that is gone. Dreams are smashed, hope is the battered victim of anger, peace is smothered by sorrow.

The close companion of failure is fear. As one new divorcee observed, "Fear of all the responsibility of having to raise two children (and thus, fear of more failure). Fear of being rejected. Fear of not being loved. Fear that no one would accept me, or, if they did accept me that they wouldn't accept my children. And some of my experiences confirmed my fears, because so many people reacted to me out of fears of their own. Many really *couldn't* accept me because of my circumstances. But, more importantly, I couldn't accept myself. I had such a small view of God and His grace and love for me."[9]

Divorce is the kind of failure that the theologians call sin. It is a sin against God, against His highest purpose for human life, against each other in the fractured relationship, and, most of all, against the children. In the stress of developing a compassionate ministry to those who have been divorced it is tempting to overlook this biblical truth.

However, it is incomplete until you add that divorce is a sin that can be forgiven. The apostle John records the incident where a woman "caught in adultery" was brought to Jesus (John 8:3, NIV). This moral misdeed was justification not only for divorce, but also death, under Jewish law.

With the gentleness that reflected His compassionate humanity, "Jesus bent down and started to write on the ground with his finger. When they kept questioning him, he straightened up and said to them, 'If any of you is without sin, let him begin stoning her'" (John 8:6-7, NIV).

Jesus was the only sinless one in the angry crowd surrounding the subdued woman. By His own standards He was the only one who qualified to pick up a heavy rock and initiate the execution of this sinner.

But He did not do it!

The rocks lay untouched in the dust. The accusers grew silent.

When they had all left without filing a formal complaint, Jesus, standing alone with the woman, said to her, "Go now and leave your life of sin" (8:11, NIV).

It seems reasonable to suppose that if Christ can forgive, then we, too, have that same wonderful privilege.

The prevalence of divorce in the church opens up two additional concerns: (1) The ground rules for fellowship for a person separated from his or her spouse and not legally divorced, and (2) The question of remarriage.

76

A. The Ground Rules of Fellowship

The church, and the individual members of the single adult group, have an obligation to give careful attention to appropriate conduct lest vulnerable persons be hurt. One experienced minister to single adults provides these guidelines:

—when one is not free to marry, one is not free to date.
—when one is not free to marry, he should inform others of his "separated" status.
—when one is not free to marry, he is probably vulnerable to attention to persons of the opposite sex.
—when one is not free to marry, all heterosexual encounters and conversations need to be in group settings and never in one-to-one settings.[10]

B. The Question of Remarriage

It is not within the scope of this study to expand the boundaries of either biblical knowledge or ecclesiastical action on the issue of the remarriage of divorced persons. It is enough, at this point, to note that regardless of the stated position of the church, most divorced persons remarry. Depending on their religious affiliation, they remarry either with or without the blessing of their church.

But they remarry.

The significant thing is that they are people in need, people who are searching for new friends and the strength to succeed where they have failed. These injured people need the healing ministry of the church. The warmth and love of God's people, as ministers of His grace, can interrupt the ugly cycle of anger and fear. They can provide an oasis of authentic friendship that offers the prospect of peace and forgiveness. During this period of crisis and readjustment these newly remarried people are often more open to the church than at any other time in their adult lives. Patience, love, and the acceptance of them as valuable persons is paramount. These people represent one of the greatest opportunities for ministry and evangelism in the church today.

II. DEATH—THOSE THAT REMAIN

Moses came down from the thundering mountain to announce to the people of the Exodus that God was establishing a new social order. The foundation stones of that new society were proclaimed to be 10 new commandments regulating social behavior. The great lawgiver then presented to the people a long list of ordinances designed by God to help a slave nation make the transition to freedom and self-government.

In the midst of that proclamation, Moses paused to remind the people of the kind of God they had followed out of Egypt into the desert on the way to the Promised Land. "For the Lord your God is the God of gods and the Lord of lords, the great, the mighty, and the awesome God who does not show partiality, nor take a bribe" (Deut. 10:17, NASB):

Those who listened that fateful day could hardly have been prepared for what immediately followed as their leader continued to talk about the nature and actions of God. "He executes justice for the orphan and the widow," Moses affirmed (10:18, NASB). Thus it is not surprising to hear him instruct the people a little later, "You shall not pervert the justice due an . . . orphan, nor take a widow's garment in pledge" (Deut. 24:17, NASB).

Compassion and concern for those who had been suddenly singled by death was expressed very early in the Bible. As the Jewish Law found fuller and more detailed expression, the rights and privileges of widows were carefully defined. The Law specified the manner in which they were to be sustained and protected by the family and the larger community that surrounded them. From the beginning, and for reasons that are obvious, the widow has been extremely visible. Widowers were less common, for the Jewish culture mandated marriage and a succession of wars kept the unmarried women decidedly in the majority. Perhaps even the polygamy that was allowed in the early portions of the sacred historical record are a concession to the need to care for the widows and the fatherless children.

This positive attitude toward widows continued into the early days of the New Testament Church. In fact, the first formal organization in the Church was designed to assist widows in trouble. In order that fair and equal treatment would be given to both Greek and Jewish widows, the apostles instructed the Infant Church to select seven men "full of the Spirit and of wisdom" for the task (Acts 6: 3, NASB).

James reflects this concern when he writes, "This is pure and undefiled religion in the sight of our God and Father, to visit orphans and widows in their distress, and to keep oneself unstained by the world" (Jas. 1:17, NASB). Clearly there was no prejudice against these "single without choice" people in the biblical account.

Widows, and widowers to a lesser degree, continue to be among the most visible single adults in the church. They are treated with compassion rather than the prejudice the divorced must face. They are considered to be the unfortunate victims of life's tragic reality.

Certainly it cannot be denied that death is a reality. As soon as a person is born he is old enough to die. In the moment that a young couple exchange marital vows they qualify as candidates for the ranks of those who can be singled without choice. Since few couples die at exactly the same moment, there shall continually be those that remain after the death of their mate.

This is not age-related, though obviously the problem increases as people grow older. Widows outnumber divorced women four to one, while widowers outnumber divorced men two to one. Most of them are older than the divorced people in our society. An overwhelming majority, four-fifths of those who remain unmarried after the death of their spouse, are women. The reason is not hard to find. The average American wife outlives her husband by about seven years. Consequently this group is largely female, with most of them having passed their 55th birthday. Thus, while the problem is not necessarily age-related, it is primarily a problem of older people.

For reasons that seem obvious, the church more readily accepts the remarriage of widowed people than that of the divorced. Studies show that widowed adults usually marry other widowed people. Probably because they share many common experiences and find it easier to relate to each other. There is no "proper" length of time that should transpire before the remarriage of widowed persons. Of significantly greater importance, however, is the need for the compassionate emotional support of the widowed so that they do not marry unwisely in search of someone who cares for them in their time of sorrow.

Emotionally, those who have experienced singleness by either death or divorce have much in common. They know loneliness, perhaps guilt, certainly the pressure of financial dislocation, social readjustment, and sexual frustration. While death is never easy, even when death is a release from the agony of unrelieved suffering, death may be easier than divorce.*

---

*By Death or Divorce, It Hurts to Lose, by Amy Ross Young, is a poignant account of this human situation. She skillfully weaves the narrative of her life through two marriages and the tumultuous experience

Yet those who are suddenly singled by death face a unique set of challenges. Probably the most difficult to handle are the restrictions that grow out of society's traditional attitudes toward the widowed.

The most difficult to face is the pressure to artificially shorten the period of grief. Friends in the church swarm around the bereaved partner, almost smothering him or her with expressions of affection and macaroni casseroles. This initial support during the period of shock, when a person has neither the strength nor the desire to prepare an adequate meal, is extremely helpful. The influx of relatives from distant places would make the funeral period intolerable without the provision of food and help from friends.

Unfortunately, however, as soon as the relatives leave, the home of the bereaved is doubly quiet. People no longer phone or visit. Behind the drawn shades of both home and heart is an increasingly lonely person as the former ties are suddenly cut and they are forced to form a new life without the support of either their loved one or friends. Sometimes people need someone just to cry with them, or to sit quietly in the dark. It is much easier to bake casseroles than it is to listen, but there comes a time when people need a friend more than a meal—and tragically, both disappear too quickly.

Perhaps it is because we do not know how to handle another's grief. Or, could it be that their encounter with death makes us feel too vulnerable to be comfortable? At any rate, we exert pressure on the bereaved to shorten their period of grief for our benefit, not theirs. One widow said, "My friends at the church say, 'be strong,' without realiz-

---

that followed. Her first marriage was terminated suddenly when her 32-year-old husband was killed in an auto accident; her second died slowly, ending in divorce. A deeply committed Christian, she shares the struggle that has brought her to a place of personal victory.

ing that it takes all my strength just to get out of bed in the morning."

Add to this the cultural pressure to remain single for a "proper" period of time out of "respect for the deceased." While this is fading in many places, it is still a sufficiently powerful force to cause unnecessary heartache and lonesomeness for many a person who has lost their partner. It could well be that fewer people would marry unwisely on the rebound from an emotional upheaval if their lives were filled with the joy and laughter that comes from being in the company of happy Christian friends.

It is estimated that the average widow uses 80 percent of her financial resources during the first 18 months following her husband's death. The largest single expenditure, obviously, is for the funeral. Sometimes money is dissipated in a futile attempt to run from reality. Unable to face the fact of singleness and the emptiness of the new, broken life, the widowed one attempts to buy a new lifestyle. Generally, this is not only expensive, but tragically unsuccessful. Peace will come only when a person has the courage to stop and face the past as well as the future. Here, again, the Christian friend who has the wisdom to be available without being intrusive can be a redemptive minister of God's healing grace.

Financial readjustment, and perhaps major dislocation, will be a part of the recovery period for many widowed people. They may become the targets for unscrupulous promoters who prey on the weak. Elderly people, especially, are often the victims of religious con artists.

Social readjustment is inextricably interwoven with the need to develop a new self-awareness apart from the former spouse. One widow observed, "Here I was, having to make all the choices and decisions on my own, and I wasn't even sure of my identity. A nagging thought persisted, and I kept asking myself, 'Who am I?' For 30 years

I had been half of a team, and now I felt as if half of me were gone."[11] Understanding friends will aid through compassion and gentle nudging. The past must not be erased, but it must be kept in the past. New goals and accompanying new skills will pull a person into the future out of the morass of self-pity faster than the best collection of well-meant advice.

One minister to single adults offers this list of practical "helps" that will encourage these individuals to move out on their own.

1. Make available any legal aid or financial advice as deemed necessary.

2. If possible, encourage the widowed person to remain in the same living quarters for a period of time—not less than three months and preferably more than one year.

3. Assume a long life ahead, and postpone parceling out material possessions to one's family.

4. Provide some healthy avenues of service through the church so the widowed person's need to give love is channeled in a good way.

5. Maintain a channel of communication to encourage participation with the single adult activities when widowed persons feel inclined to participate.

6. Give the responsibility of caring back to the people in the congregation. Help them be shepherds to this often-neglected group.[12]

Reentry into normal living is possible. Frances Robinson writes of her own recovery from the death of her husband,

> After a while I found I had learned several things. I learned to like my new title of widow. My new identity had been revealed and was becoming clearer. I was able to begin again in my business career and to continue to improve my avocation of writing. I discovered some

lonely folks who wanted visitors and found ways to help in my church. My life has been given new purpose. I am learning to live alone—one day at a time—and am enjoying it.[13]

The widowed need to be challenged to make new beginnings, which may, or may not include remarriage. Most of them are very reluctant to accept singleness as a necessary life-style. They resent the tragedy that has robbed them of their best and forced them into a lonely life. What a tremendous opportunity for the church to provide the atmosphere of love that will enable the individual to grow through the experience of sorrow.

III. The Bible and Human Sexuality

Does this subject seem inappropriate in a book on developing a ministry to single adults? Then most likely you are married. The fact is that it is one of the major problems Christian single adults are forced to face. Not that they have filthy minds, but they, too, live in a sex-saturated society where rules for moral behavior are collapsing.

Generally speaking, the church has not been much help to single adults in their struggle to live a clean life in a morally corrupt world. Christians have not handled the subject of sex with much finesse. Our silence has made the subject appear to be dirty. To many single adults, evangelical Christians seem to want a world that is asexual. We appear to be embarrassed to admit that sex is pleasurable for fear that we will be labeled as perverted. One young man, a Christian single, observed, "Most married couples in the church, when leading a session on 'Sex and the Single Adult,' have only enough courage to talk about sex from the neck up!"

This much is axiomatic: no study on single adult ministry is complete without considering this issue; no successful single adult program in the church can ignore the impact of sex on its participants.

> There is a danger of the Christian fellowship becoming so sanctimonious that those with deep, unresolved problems are frightened into silence or hypocrisy. This is especially true in the area of sex . . . A significant number of seemingly innocent Christian women wrestle with problems of homosexuality, immorality, rape, and sexual molestation. The church has a responsibility to minister forgiveness, new life and healing to such women. Only as such problems and anxieties are brought out into the open and resolved through sensitive counseling and good teaching from a biblical perspective will the single woman grow as a whole person.[14]

This can be broadened to include single men, also.

The sexual adjustments and frustrations are even greater for the formerly married. The basic, powerful, human drives that had found legitimate fulfillment in marriage have been cut off, abruptly. The body cries out for the same kind of physical reassurance that had been an intimate part of the married life. The world says that it is acceptable to find sexual fulfillment in casual relationships—sex as recreation, and re-creation. The church subscribes, properly, to the biblical ideal—intimacy only in marriage. The conspiracy of silence within the church on this volatile subject tends to increase the problems many have in adjusting their human hungers to meet their actual situation. It may serve to explain why so many of the formerly married remarry so quickly.

Paul Tournier identifies four distinct attitudes toward sex:

First, are those who devaluate sexuality, reducing it to the level of a glandular function, an instinctive, biological act.

Second, the pleasure-seekers who deify sexuality, overestimating its importance and judging all of life from this perspective.

Third, are the ones who consider sex necessary but contemptible.

Fourth, the biblical view: a look "at sex through what I would like to call the eyes of biblical attitude. These would admit that sex is biological in some sense. They could agree that sex is immensely pleasurable. But, bypassing the third attitude altogether, they go on to another point as yet unmade: that the fulness and wholeness of sexual experience is the *result* of a relationship, not the beginning or the entirety of one."[15]

It is this biblical picture that must be given as the authentic message from the church and seen modeled by the Christian couples in the fellowship. With it will go a conscious rejection of our preconceived notions. We will accept Christian single adults as being as careful in matters of public and private morality as married couples. This trust will be reflected in our relationships and will be revealed in our speech. We will be careful not to presume moral sin among single adults, as is evident in the incident that went like this:

A young lady said, "I have a new roommate."

A friend replied, "Is it a boy or a girl?"

She was furious as she responded, "You wouldn't say to a married woman who was a Christian, 'Who are you committing adultery with today?'!"

Human sexuality was God's idea; do not blame it on the devil. It is good because it is the gift of God. As God continually observed the process of creation, the only thing He labeled as "not good" was that man was lonely. God solved this problem by creating a female, not another male. The intimate relationship between man and woman is an old idea, and it is a good one, not an evil one. The biblical concept of sex is one of completeness, not ecstacy, or recreation, or re-creation. Nor was it intended to be used as an antidote for loneliness, or to prop up the ego of an insecure person.

When God created woman, He could have made humanity unisex and arranged for the propagation of the race by some other means. But obviously He wanted there to be a difference between the sexes. Eve was created, not primarily for child-bearing, but to remedy Adam's loneliness. Their intimacy was not only for reproduction, but also for enjoyment and fulfillment. The full implications of this relationship are called honorable in the Bible (Heb. 13:4). "The message of biblical sexuality is then one of commitment. It demands a beginning of commitment and a continuity of commitment. Without that unreserved fidelity to one another, 'knowing' will be reduced to 'lying with.' With it, the genius of commitment is affirmed, and our very being fulfills that for which God has made us."[16]

The spin-off of this is that this special kind of intimacy is to be confined to marriage. The Christian answer to sexual problems among single adults dare not, however, be limited to a simple authoritarian statement. It will provide opportunities for study and spiritual growth coupled with an understanding of the grace of God that gives guidance and offers forgiveness. Not much will be solved by denying the problem nor refusing to consider the issues. As has been noted, "The gift of God is the control, not the annihilation of the drive." A thoroughly biblical study of human sexuality will provide the Christian single adult with the spiritual resources to combat the pressures of our erotic society. Both intimacy as recreation, and intimacy between people of the same sex are clearly denied in the Bible. Single adults will welcome a clear biblical base on which to build a strong Christian answer when they face these crucial issues.

Something to Discuss or Do

1. What are the three stages of divorce?

2. Why does divorce cause a greater identity crisis for women than it does for men?

3. What is the one overwhelming emotion experienced by the newly divorced?

4. Why is it necessary to have some "ground rules of fellowship" for a single adult group—especially for those who have "separated" status?

5. How should the church community respond to those who remarry after divorce?

6. What are some of the problems common to both widowed and divorced persons?

7. How does the church community unknowingly make a widowed person's adjustments difficult?

8. How can the church be more helpful to the widowed as they begin a new life-style?

9. Why are many single adults in the church struggling with problems concerning their sexuality?

10. What is the biblical view of sex?

CHAPTER 6

Getting Started
in the Local Church

Dear Gene,

I have been a widow for 10 years. I feel, and have felt for some time the need for a special ministry to us singles. This need is growing daily with the divorce rate increasing as it is. We are a needy people—we feel a deep need for Christian fellowship, friendship, and other church oriented activities.

I feel I have personally come a long way, with just God and myself. But, you see, 10 years alone is quite a long time. I see people every day of my life who are single for one reason or another. They are lonely, some are even desperate. If these people can be reached with Christian love at the time they need help most, it will keep many people from straying from God, and bring many back to Him.

I feel the church has failed to provide guidance and help for the single adults of every age. We need the church to help us.

Sincerely,
Helen

This gentle, but pleading letter from Helen (that's not her real name), highlights two important facets of any ministry to single adults. First, in most places, such a ministry is either ineffective or nonexistent. Second, single adults know that they are single. It is the dominating fact of their lives. They are reminded of their singleness more often than couples remember their married status. This has both a minus and a plus factor.

It is a minus if the church continues to ignore this significant and growing minority. Their singleness then becomes a recurring temptation to find a church that will surround and support them with care and love. It is a plus for the church that is willing to make an honest attempt to help them in all the areas of life where they feel lonely and inadequate. When a single adult attends a meeting designed for singles he is willingly accepting society's stigma. He is consciously testifying that he is in a misunderstood and neglected minority. He is saying, "I have some major unmet needs in my life or I would not be here. Can you help me?" This act of confidence in your church can be the opportunity for tremendous blessing.

It is a strange paradox that such a minority should be "singled out" for special ministry by separating them from the majority. Should this happen? Or, would it be better to integrate them into classes and social groups without regard to their marital status?

Let it be noted that the ideal would be for people to be treated as valuable persons without respect to the identifying factor that sets them off from the majority, be it race, color, national origin, religious beliefs, or marital status. When a local church comes to the place that an individual is made to feel comfortable and "at home" even though he represents a minority, then at that time, there is no need for a specialized ministry to people who differ from the majority.

But for most of our churches, and for many of the people who attend, that day is still in the future. Single adult

Sunday school classes, social activities, and special singles' events are going to continue to be a vital part of the church program for the foreseeable future.

Care must be taken that a single adult ministry is not considered as a ministry to the underprivileged or some sort of a "halfway" house between disaster and marriage. Single adults are mature persons who, while possessing special needs, are normal people with all the potential for growth God has given anyone. A successful singles' program will probably begin to work itself out of a job as the people are assimilated into the mainstream of the church. That is, it would, except that successful programs have a way of attracting the lonesome and the unattached in the community. Success in this venture, as in everything we do in the church, only increases our opportunities.

I. The Time to Start

How many single adults do you need in your church before you begin to develop a ministry to single adults? 10? 30? 50? Perhaps we can rephrase the question. How many Africans were members of the church before Harmon Schmelzenbach journeyed by foot and oxcart from the southern tip of Africa to Swaziland? How many Methodists before John Wesley; how many Protestants before Martin Luther; how many Christians before Calvary?

The historic religious movements that have changed the course of history were not dependent on the identification of majority support in a Gallup Poll. Nor were they concerned with the preservation of the "status quo." They willingly cut loose from the traditional, and therefore safe, pursuit of happiness in religious expression and launched into the unknown.

Thus, also, a church's entry into a significant ministry with single adults. It is a kind of missionary adventure of

91

the most significant proportions. The missionary does not go to new lands for Christ in order to obtain support for the parent institution. Evangelism and institutional survival are not necessarily related. Evangelism has a much higher goal as expressed by a missionary serving the Lord in Venezuela, "The attitude of the missionary should not be that of one who goes to others to get anything, whether followers, or merit, or rewards, or praise, or appreciation. It should be that of one who gives, who gives because he must give, who learned to give from the One who 'so loved the world that he gave his only begotten Son.'"[1]

Begin by helping your church understand the large number of single adults in your community that do not attend church anywhere. Help them see the subtle changes that need to take place to insure that a single will feel welcome. Few active members of your congregation are aware how completely the married-couple-with-children-living-at-home has become the norm of Christian life in America. Provide them with opportunities to expand their vision of "Family Ministry" to include those who do not fit neatly into that cultural framework. Encourage them to take the big step of missionary adventure that comes with the opportunity to begin to minister to single adults.

Ultimately, regardless of how many, or how few, single adults there are in your church, a ministry to them will begin in the heart of just one person. Join together in prayer that the Lord will begin to lay the burden of this ministry on your hearts until effective leadership is called to this crucial task.

II. THE PLACE TO START

Start with single adults, not married couples.

This may seem simplistic, but since so few single adults are in leadership positions in the church, it is easy to plan for them rather than with them. They do not want you to make a special place for them in the church; they want to become an integral part of the church. Involve them in the planning from the very beginning. After all, they are adults, not big teenagers.

A. First, Identify the Singles in Your Congregation

If your church is an average church, there are more single adults in your fellowship than you may have realized.

A good way to begin is to include a card in the Sunday bulletin asking for information relative to the beginning of a ministry to single adults in your church. Ask all the never-married, and the formerly-married, either by death or divorce, to complete a simple questionnaire. This form should include, in addition to name and address, etc., a place for them to check their approximate age (20-30; 31-40; 41 and above, for example). Do not overlook the singles above 40 years of age. In many churches they are the most active single adult group in the congregation. Also include a space on the card for them to express an opinion or share an idea.

Follow this with an "idea" meeting. Do not assume that you know what their needs are. Ask them. A major department store has this motto, "Only the customer knows when he is satisfied." It is the same with singles. Only they really know when their interests and needs are being met.

Announce this "idea" meeting far enough in advance so that every single adult can arrange his schedule to be present. If possible, hold this meeting in a home rather than the church. The more relaxed atmosphere may make it easier for some of them to express their hopes and dreams for the new organization.

It is probably too early to elect officers at this meeting. Wait until you have a better idea of the form the group will take. However, you will want to appoint a secretary pro tem so that you do not lose any ideas, and it would be in order to appoint a temporary chairman to lead the discussion. Two of your concerned singles can give the ministry a big push at this point.

It is extremely important, at this stage, that the group feels the privilege to be creative. It is quite likely that they will chart a course different from the one married couples would design for them. Their lack of family commitments gives them the freedom to develop a more flexible program than married couples are free to follow. Trust them! And trust the Holy Spirit to lead them. This may be the most difficult challenge for the leaders in the local church as the single adult ministry has its beginning.

B. Have a Planning Session

Encourage the planning session to establish some goals and objectives for the group. These do not need to be complex, but should answer questions like these: "Where are we?" "Where do we want to be in six months?" "How are we going to get there?" After some kind of steering committee or council has been formed, they will want to give more attention to guidelines for growth. Here are some items to be considered:

1. *Plan for personal spiritual growth.* Design your program to lead every individual to a place of personal commitment to Christ.

2. *Remember the very real social needs of singles.* They are looking for activities to fill up the many lonely hours with something more wholesome than a singles' bar or a singles' dance.

3. *Do not allow the group to become heavily conditioned toward marriage.* A singles group should be much

more than an inexpensive religiously oriented dating service for lonely adults.

Of course, couples will be formed, and many will get married. For them, plan an "Alumni Class" for one quarter in your Sunday school and deal with the important challenge every young married couple faces.

4. *Encourage the single adults to live **now**.* Far too many singles are in a "holding pattern." They are doing nothing until the time comes when they get married and have someone with whom they can share their experiences.

C. Elect Officers

As soon as the organization begins to take shape, elect officers for six-month periods. These short-term elections will be invigorating for your group. Use a nominating committee in preparation for the election. It is important that the right people be elected. In every church there are "negative" single adults who have a pessimistic outlook because of unhappy personal experiences. These people can kill your group before it gets started if they emerge as the leaders.

D. Relate to the Church

The singles ministry in your church will become a part of the Adult Department of the Board of Christian Life. The director of Adult Ministries and the pastor are the two key people with whom you will want to work and maintain a "working" relationship. Keep your group closely related to the church for the mutual benefit of both your group and the church. Singles do not need more isolation; they need to be encouraged to become an integral part of the Body of Christ.

In cooperation with the leaders just named, the single adult program will be defined. This will include the selection of study materials for the Sunday school classes, the recruitment of leaders and teachers, and the development of a well-rounded program. Often the question is asked, "Can married couples serve as teachers in single adult classes or Bible studies?"

Of course they can! In fact, a happily married couple can model a successful Christian marriage as well as mature Christian living. This can give the program a special dimension. Of far more importance than the marital status of the leaders is the awareness of the interests and needs of single adults and the willingness to move vigorously to help meet those needs.

III. Keeping the Program Alive

Let's face it. It is easier to start programs than it is to maintain them.

A few years ago I sat at lunch with one of the nine young men who had launched a new concept in teen evangelism called "Youth for Christ." Now in comfortable midlife, he reflected on those days when concerned Christians spawned a wide variety of programs to reach teenagers with the message of Christ. Those were exciting times to be involved in a ministry to teens.

Once again the church is pioneering new territory, this time to take the story of salvation to single adults. Many churches are taking their first tentative steps across the border of this new frontier.

The response can be both challenging and frustrating. Sometimes, quite honestly, it is discouraging. On review, it is apparent that often the result for a feeling of failure grows out of a misconception of the dimensions of the church's ministry to single adults.

The first step in many churches has been to cluster single adults into convenient units for group activity as we packaged our successful teen programs. But it is not possible, nor desirable, to try and "herd" single adults. There is far more diversity among them than is found in the teen years. It is true that they may lack a meaningful social life. But they need much more: they are seeking redemptive answers to challenging personal problems resulting from loss or rejection.

The ministry of the church to single adults will never follow the pattern of the explosion of teen ministries following World War II. However, a patient awareness of their needs, and a willingness to adapt our program to meet them where they are, will make it possible for the church to fulfill its mission to them.

A. Start with the Sunday School

Organize a class for single adults. As the group grows in attendance you may want to divide along age and/or interest lines. Obviously, a grouping of people along lines of common interest will aid their study and spiritual growth. The divisions that were suggested earlier, in Chapter 1, will give guidance here.

In cooperation with the single adults and the director of Adult Ministries, plan a curriculum that will challenge the best of those who attend. Along with the study of the Bible as it is presented in the regular Sunday school lessons, special short courses on key subjects can be very helpful. Here are some appropriate themes:

—coping with divorce
—building self-esteem
—preparation for marriage
—successful single parenting
—financial planning
—love, sex, and dating

—the challenge of the widowed

—how to handle grief

Short courses, four to six weeks in length, will open up the possibility of involving everyone in these specialized studies. For example, it is not unusual for single parents to accept a teaching responsibility in the Children's Department because they want their children to be in Sunday school and they are uncomfortable in the adult class. By planning these short courses far enough in advance you could release such a person for a month or so to attend a class that would help them grow as a Christian, or gain new insights on how to be a better parent, for example.

Select a unique meeting place. Should the single adult class meet at the church, or at a nearby restaurant or clubhouse? There is no universal answer to this question. However, the answer should be in keeping with the agreed-upon goals and objectives of the group. There are many singles who are very reluctant to attend church. A religious meeting on neutral ground is less threatening to them. Some excellent groups meet in coffeehouses or restaurants near the church. One such group, meeting in an inn, printed tickets which they distributed to advertise their meeting time and place. The tickets were cleverly titled, "Inn-Sight." An ample supply gave the participants a simple, effective way to invite others to the meeting. Sunday school leaders will want to counsel with the single adult leaders in deciding on the best meeting place in order to reach the established goals.

Bible study for singles usually is most helpful when it is scheduled, on a regular basis, in a private home. Some kind of light refreshments at the beginning will set an informal tone to the meeting, communicating warmth and love. Encourage people to get acquainted with one another. As you move into the Bible study, remember to involve them in the learning process. Focus your study, not only on what the Bible says, but also on how they may apply it to their personal life situation. Encourage the single adults to make positive life changes based on the principles they discover in God's Word.

Some singles' groups that meet in a restaurant on Sunday morning, come early enough for breakfast and follow with a Bible study. Special care is taken to make visitors welcome. They are assigned to individual hosts, or hostesses, who invite them to spend the day with them. This includes the Bible study, church, lunch, a planned afternoon activity, and the evening service. This Bible study is always dismissed so that the participants can be "on time" for the morning worship service. Visitors, of course, are given a special invitation to join them in worship.

B. Maintain Flexibility

Establish a process whereby the study curriculum in both Sunday school and the Bible studies is regularly reviewed. This will insure that the program is speaking to the needs and interests of those who are in attendance. As noted earlier, this needs to be a cooperative effort between single adult leaders and the local director of Adult Ministries.

One California congregation has worked out a unique format for their weeknight meetings. The program runs three Fridays each month. The first Friday features a seminar. They have considered topics like "The Roommate Dilemma," "One-Parent Families," "Twenty-five Ways to Stay Lonely," and "Divorce and Remarriage."

A potluck dinner, with entertainment, games, and fellowship, is scheduled for every second Friday.

The third Friday is open.

Bible study is the focus for the fourth Friday.[2]

C. Organize Support Groups

Obviously, singles do not have the family support that married couples experience. The passing of the years and a variety of crisis situations tend to further isolate them from others. The creation of support groups for caring, listening, providing assistance, and the sharing of fun and fellowship can be very helpful. They provide the single adult an "extended family."

Both the size and length of these groups can vary according to need. Five to eight people in each group is a workable size, allowing it to fit nicely into most apartments and giving room for growth. These groups may stay in existence for a few weeks to several months. An occasional reshuffling of the groups will add interest and discourage the formation of cliques.

D. Design an Attractive Social Program

Earlier in this chapter we noted that a singles program must consist of far more than a preplanned social time. There are challenges to face, problems to solve, and spiritual gifts that need to be developed.

Yet the church dare not overlook the fellowship needs of single adults. The competition from the world for their relaxed time and entertainment dollar is immense. Far too often, Christian singles have reluctantly attended activities of marginal value because there "was no place else to go." A young man, returning from a weekend spiritual retreat with a group of Christian single adults, said, "I wish I could attend something like this every weekend. But, since I can't, I know what I'll do next Saturday night. I'll go to the dance, because that's the only place in our town where you can meet other single adults. I know it ain't right, but what's a guy to do?"

We would agree: it ain't right! Hopefully, soon one of the churches in his small town will expand its vision and ministry to include him. Perhaps we ought not to expend our energy in condemning the actions of people like him until we have made every conceivable effort to provide wholesome entertainment opportunities for single adults.

"What are your hobbies? What do you do to relax?" the doctor asked as he reviewed Brad's chart.

"Hobbies?" Brad laughed bitterly. "You've got to be kidding! I'm new in town and just going through a divorce. What would I do for fun?"[3]

Have you ever asked yourself, "If I were a single adult this Friday night, what would I do for entertainment that would be in keeping with my Christian convictions?"

Many Christian single adults are scheduling regular times to eat together. Often this is on Sunday after the morning worship service. For others, it is on a weeknight. The ground rules are simple, but rigidly applied:

1. Every person brings one item for the meal: a casserole, salad, etc.

2. Each person brings his own table service—and takes it home with him to wash. The host, or hostess, is not saddled with a massive cleanup job when it is over.

3. The meal is scheduled to begin at a specific time. No one is to arrive more than 15 minutes prior to that hour. They agree to spend just one hour together, no more. Everyone is required to leave in 60 minutes. The rationale is simply this: you have to eat somewhere. Whether you stay at home, or go to a restaurant, it will take most of an hour to eat. Under these conditions you are not taking any extra time for the evening meal, and you get to spend it with friends. The 60-minute time limit insures that it does not steal time from other planned activities. It is not a social evening, but a "family" meal together.

Other singles groups plan occasional "Oasis" weekends where they go to a resort, or camping place, as a "Singles' Family." This gives them the joy of sharing new experiences with friends. As with couples who attend retreats, or vacation together, the highest and best of Christian living is exemplified in their behavior.

Holidays are especially difficult for those single adults who are living at some distance from their family. The loneliness is intensified during those periods. What a wonderful opportunity for the church to plan a big communal dinner at the church and invite everyone who wishes to join. This, also, will prove to be an excellent time for both single adults and married couples to share the time together.

Singles would also welcome the chance to be an occasional part of a "normal" family evening. To be invited over on a Friday night just to watch television, pop popcorn, and eat apples with a family may not seem like much to the married, but it will be a delightful experience for the one who is denied this simple pleasure.

E. Arrange Adequate Financing of the Program

At first, as with any important new venture, the Church Board may need to budget sufficient funds to launch the program. When the group has gained some working vitality, they should be able to finance most of the things they wish to do as single adults.

Occasionally, however, it may be necessary to purchase equipment or subsidize other aspects of the program to open up the possibility of continued growth. When this need arises, it should not trouble the church. We provide this kind of financial assistance to other key parts of the church's ministry on a regular basis. For example, we do not ask the choir to pay all of its expenses in order to have the privilege to sing for the church on Sunday morning.

F. Publicize the Program

Let the community know what you are doing. Keep them informed. There are many single adults in your community who do not wish to be involved in the non-Christian activities attractively packaged and heavily promoted in your city. They will respond to your advertisement.

Keep your publicity thoroughly Christian. Not that you would be tempted to present the work of Christ in a sinful way, but resist the temptation to present it in a secular way. Insure that every ad clearly reveals that this is a "Christian singles" organization. This will help discourage those "hustlers" who hop from group to group with no other object than to meet unattached girls.

Above all else, do not put the publicity for your singles' activities on the religious page of your newspaper. That is not where the singles are looking. Put it on the entertainment page, where it will catch their eye.

One creative single's group, having exhausted their publicity budget, were forced to cancel their newspaper advertising. They printed up a large supply of colorful cards advertising their organization, its time and place of meeting, etc. These were made available to the group. When they went shopping, to the laundromat, or any place providing free advertising, they would slip one of these cards into the rack. In their city, they found that it generated more response than the more expensive newspaper ads, at considerably less cost.

IV. INVOLVE SINGLE ADULTS IN THE TOTAL PROGRAM

Single adults can be Christians, too! As Christians they want to have the opportunity to develop and use their spiritual gifts in the work of the Kingdom. As their leaders are given visibility by appointment and election to key positions in the church, the image of the Christian single will grow immeasurably.

Along with this, provide opportunities for the singles to meet the church. Do not segregate them to a back room on Friday night. One successful single adult Sunday school class plans a social with the senior adults at least once a quarter. The maturity of one group combined with the enthusiasm of the other creates a pleasant experience for both. Others have combined Bible study during Sunday school of such diverse groups, for a short period of time. This cross-generational study can be extremely invigorating. Social activities that bring together married couples and single adults can also expand the Christian vision of both.

When Christian singles have achieved something of value or contributed special service to the church, give them public recognition. Remember, they do not have a spouse or family at home to commend them on their contributions to the Kingdom. They will welcome your encouragement.

A successful minister to singles makes these observations:

What Doesn't Get Singles into the Church:

1. Folk Services
2. New liturgy forms
3. Coffeehouses
4. Films, activities
5. Debates or discussions
6. Dating service

What Does Get Singles into the Church:

1. A pastor and people who genuinely care and are concerned

2. Pure gospel orientation which you can get nowhere but in the church
3. A feeling of being accepted and belonging
4. Opportunity to grow in faith and knowledge of God
5. Opportunity to express one's personal opinions and experience open exchange
6. Christian fellowship[4]

Churches that are successful in reaching and ministering to singles strive to build this atmosphere of acceptance. Acceptance and love are the key ingredients. Perhaps that is just another way of saying, "compassion." Compassion means to participate in feeling rather than simply viewing the scene as a spectator. Compassion is not the emotion of the weak. It is the property of the strong, the vital, Christian emotion of love in action.

SOMETHING TO DISCUSS OR DO

1. What two facets of the church's ministry to single adults are revealed in Helen's letter?
—Are they a minus or a plus?

2. What unspoken message is given when a single adult attends a meeting designed exclusively for singles?

3. Should single adults be "singled out"?

4. When should you start a single adult group in a local church?

5. With whom should you begin planning for such a group?

6. What are the first steps to starting a ministry among single adults?

7. How can you keep the singles' program alive?

Reference Notes

CHAPTER 1

1. Nicholas B. Christoff, *Saturday Night, Sunday Morning* (New York: Harper & Row Publishers, 1978), pp. 2-3.

2. Britton Wood, *Single Adults Want to Be the Church, Too* (Nashville: Broadman Press, 1977), p. 39.

3. *Single i,* October, 1977, p. 3.

4. Christoff, *Saturday Night,* p. 5.

5. *Single i,* January, 1978, p. 2.

6. Gary Collins, *It's OK to Be Single* (Waco, Tex: Word Books, Inc., 1976), p. 25.

CHAPTER 2

1. Earl A. Grollman, ed., *Explaining Divorce to Children* (Boston: Beacon Press, 1969), p. 4.

2. Christoff, *Saturday Night,* pp. 7, 8-9.

3. *Ibid.,* p. 13.

4. Wood, *Single Adults,* p. 20.

5. *Solo,* June-July, 1978.

6. Newsletter, Women's Aldersgate Fellowship, Winter, 1978.

7. Collins, *It's OK,* p. 11.

8. Wood, *Single Adults,* pp. 22-23.

9. Virginia Watts, *The Single Parent* (Old Tappan, N.J.: Fleming H. Revell, Co., 1976), p. 15.

10. *Ibid.,* p. 18.

11. *Single i,* October, 1976, p. 3.

12. *Single i,* November 4, 1972, p. 2.

CHAPTER 3

1. Denny Rydberg, ed., *Whatever Happened to Marriage?* (Chicago: David C. Cook Publishing Co., 1976), p. 32.

CHAPTER 4

1. William Barclay, "The Letters to the Corinthians," *The Daily Study Bible* (Philadelphia: The Westminster Press, 1956) p. 68.

2. *Eerdman's Handbook to the Bible,* ed. by David Alexander (Grand Rapids: William B. Eerdmans Publishing Co., 1973), p. 592.

3. Barclay, "Corinthians," p. 66.

4. *Beacon Bible Commentary* (Kansas City: Beacon Hill Press of Kansas City, 1968), 8:379.

CHAPTER 5

1. Gary R. Collins, ed., *The Secrets of Our Sexuality* (Waco, Tex.: Word Books, 1976), p. 72.

2. Ada Lum, *Single and Human* (Downers Grove, Ill.: Inter-Varsity Press, 1977), p. 9.

3. *Single i,* September, 1976, p. 4.

4. Watts, *Single Parent,* p. 84.

5. Gary R. Collins, ed., *Make More of Your Marriage* (Waco, Tex.: Word Books, 1976), p. 7.

6. *Ibid.,* p. 101.

7. Norman Wright, *An Answer to Divorce* (Irvine, Calif.: Harvest House Publishers, 1977), p. 17.

8. *Single i,* January, 1978, p. 4.

9. *The Enlightener,* June, 1977.

10. Wood, *Single Adults,* pp. 82-83.

11. *Decision,* June, 1978.

12. Wood, *Single Adults,* p. 64.

13. *Decision,* June, 1978.

14. Collins, *It's OK,* p. 30.

15. Gordon MacDonald, *Magnificent Marriage* (Wheaton, Ill.: Tyndale House Publishers, 1976), p. 135.

16. *Ibid.,* p. 148.

CHAPTER 6

1. Christoff, *Saturday Night,* p. 11.

2. *Single i,* June, 1978, p. 1.

3. Bobbie Reed, *Developing a Single Adult Ministry* (Glendale, Calif.: International Center for Learning, 1977), p. 19.

4. Christoff, *Saturday Night,* p. 127.